DEEP CALLING DEEP

A TRAVEL NARRATIVE

Encounters with Jesus in the Gospel of John

SAM HUNTER

Deep Calling Deep
by Sam Hunter

Printed in the United States of America
ISBN (Paperback): 978-1-954943-59-9
ISBN (Hardcover): 978-1-954943-61-2

High Bridge Books titles may be purchased in bulk for educational, business, fundraising, or sales promotional use. For information, please contact High Bridge Books via www.HighBridgeBooks.com/contact.

Published in Houston, Texas by High Bridge Books.

To James Orders, deceased, who discipled me one on one, shortly after I was born again. For sixteen weeks he opened the scriptures to me and propelled me deeper into the Father's Word and his Kingdom Among Us.

To Randy McCreight, David Stone, Neel Reynolds, Cubby Culbertson and Det Bowers, who first showed me what a man sold out to Jesus looked like.

To my wife, Dina, who helped me with "what to leave in and what to leave out" and pointed out inconsistencies in my storyline. (Sometimes, to my annoyance)

Thank you, thank you, thank you, Jesus, for never giving up on me - please, never let up on me.

As the deer pants for streams of water,
so my soul pants for you, my God.
My soul thirsts for God, for the living God.
When can I go and meet with God?
My tears have been my food
day and night,
while people say to me all day long,
"Where is your God?"

Why, my soul, are you downcast?
Why so disturbed within me?
Put your hope in God,
for I will yet praise him,
my Savior and my God.

Deep calls to deep
in the roar of your waterfalls;
all your waves and breakers
have swept over me.

—Psalm 42:1-3, 5, 7
emphasis added

CONTENTS

ACKNOWLEDGMENTS

You will find in this book several teachings that I learned from my friend, Doug Greenwold. (Passed from this world)

You will also see several teachings from our friend Brad Gray.

And as always, I am influenced, even when I do not realize it, by C.S. Lewis and Oswald Chambers.

These and other acknowledgments are found at the back of the book.

INTRODUCTION

Will you join me as we begin John's Gospel? Let's first think about where John is in life, so we can better understand why John is writing and what he wants to say to us about Jesus.

John is around ninety years old. He was about seventeen or eighteen when Jesus was crucified and resurrected. So now we are some seventy years later. Seventy years is a long time to contemplate this man, Jesus. All John's friends are gone ... long gone. His brother James was beheaded fifty years ago. His dear friend Peter has been dead for thirty years, as has Paul. Both executed by the insane Nero. All the original disciples are dead.

Even Jesus' mother, Mary, for whom John had been caring all those years, has been dead for thirty years. John lives in Ephesus, in Asia, far from his beloved Israel. Jerusalem is no more – destroyed in 70 AD by the Romans. The Jews are scattered into the diaspora. Perhaps John at times felt like my dear ninety-five-year-old mother when she smiles and says, "I look in the mirror and ask, 'Who is that old woman looking back at me?'"

John has had seventy years to reflect, to ponder the essence of his Savior, his best friend, who turned his world upside down. No, right side up!

John is surrounded by men and women who never met Jesus. Is the memory of his dear, precious friend fading? Perhaps the facts are not yet fading, because the first three Gospels, Matthew, Mark and Luke, have been around for years. They are full of accurate facts and information about Jesus.

But is the Jesus whom John knew so intimately fading from view as this first century comes to a close? It is doubtful that the record of Jesus' acts and accomplishments has faded, given the well-known records from the Gospels, but what may have become more remote is the memory of the essence of Jesus - who he was, and who he is. After all, John called himself, "The disciple whom Jesus loved." Perhaps John is concerned this latest generation of Christians doesn't know, and cannot feel this intimate love that pulsated through, and outwardly from Jesus.

How would you tell the story of your best friend to those who have never met him or her? Would you add more facts and more information? Or would you want to paint a picture of the *Life* that was in them? John masterfully paints so much more than a picture; he paints for us a living portrait of Jesus.

Imagine your best friend dies. The newspaper runs his or her obituary, and a friend or two writes a letter to the editor talking about the facts of your dear friend's life. This happened when my father died. The Sumter newspaper ran a fine article about him. They interviewed his friends, and each friend had very nice things to say about Dad.

But could they capture the essence of my father? Could they fully represent the life that was Dad? No. For that, one would have to live with him, grow up with him, and experience life with him. So John, wanting to paint a picture of the essence of Jesus, starts with this: "In him was life, and that life was the light of all mankind." (John 1:4)

Life.

Jesus had Life in him. Life with a capital 'L'. Jesus had Life pulsating through him. Everyone who met him felt it. Just about everyone who met him liked him – even those who were not like him, liked him. Do you know anyone you would describe this way? Think about what words might come to mind. Energy. Positive energy. Passionate. Eager. Engaging. Encouraging. Inviting. Warm. Patient. Captivating. Unique.

Do you know him this way? Would you describe his life in you as explosive, freeing, rich, lavish, powerful, peaceful, and joy-full? If not, there is so much more awaiting you.

Those who now live the Life Jesus lived have, "found the small gate and the narrow road that leads to life – and only a few find it." (Matt. 7:1)

John wants his original readers – and the Father wants you, you, my friend, reading this right now – to know the Jesus he knew. So he writes a different kind of story. John's gospel has ninety percent new material. The first three Gospels include eighteen to twenty miracles. John includes eight. But John calls them signs, not miracles.

Signs, because signs point us to something. John wants you to see the Jesus to whom they point: this Jesus, who is the Son of God, and also this same Jesus who is his closest friend. The Jesus who so flooded his life with love that John called himself, "The disciple whom Jesus loved."

I do not think John is saying Jesus loved him more than the others. It seems impossible that Jesus could love anyone more than anyone else. And yes, this would mean he loves you as much as he loved John. Can you imagine that? This truth should cause you to sit down and contemplate the wonder of it. Do not rush by this. Jesus loves you, adores you in fact, as much as he did the great Apostle John.

I think by calling himself this "Disciple whom Jesus loved," John is conveying to us that over these last seventy years, his overwhelming memory, what made an impression ... an imprint ... an indentation in his heart and his very soul, was the way Jesus loved.

Deeply. Penetrating. Saturating. Soul-soothing love.

We will see this perfect understanding in the encounters John reveals. With Nicodemus, the up and in. With the Samaritan woman at the well, the down and out. And a host of others, all more like us than we might at first realize. This is why I am only going to follow Jesus' encounters with these various people. You can read, and please do read, all the rest in the gospel of John.

Encounters are how we gain the measure of a man. In Jesus' encounters with these select few, we will see the real-life, up close and personal, even intimate Jesus. The first three Gospel accounts give us the history of Jesus. I want to explore the mystery of Jesus. The first three accounts give us the heart of Jesus, but I want you to feel the heartbeat of Jesus.

Everyone who met him felt it. Some loved it. Some did not, because they either did not understand him, or they felt threatened by him. As we read John's Gospel we will encounter all three.

Which are you?

Think about this: God, John the Baptist, and John the disciple all stated that Jesus' mission was to destroy the work of the devil, and to deal with our sinful condition. For example:

God told Joseph to name his baby boy Jesus, "because he will save his people from their sins." (Matthew 1:21)

John the Baptist said, "Look, the Lamb of God, who takes away the sin of the world! (John 1:29)

John, our disciple, said, "The reason the Son of God appeared was to destroy the devil's work." (1 John 3:8)

But Jesus himself had a different take on his mission. He said, in essence, and please do not miss this, "The reason I have come, what compels me, my driving purpose, is for you to experience the same Life that I have with the Father – that is Life with a capital L."

Jesus stated this plainly: "I have come so that you may have life, and I am talking about life to the full!" (John 10:10 slight paraphrase)

Before I met this Jesus, so full of Life, all I had was the 'little l' life. I did not know Jesus had such a Life to give. As a matter of fact, I was pretty sure whatever life he had to give me would be boring and irrelevant, compared to my culturally-induced-cataract of silly ideas about the good life.

The good life. Ha!

I truly hope you will join us as we dig into the greatest story ever told. Why John's Gospel? Eugene Peterson best explains why:

> Matthew, Mark and Luke write like kayakers on a swiftly flowing river with occasional patches of white water.
>
> But John is more like a canoe on a quiet lake, drifting unhurriedly, paddling leisurely to take in the sights along the shoreline, noticing rock formations, observing a blue heron fishing in the rushes, pausing and drifting to sketch cloud patterns reflected in the glassy water. (Introduction to John MSG)

Jesus means it when he tells you, you, my friend, reading this right now, "I have come so that you ______________ may start today experiencing my Life to the Full – so full even to the point of overflowing." (Fill in your name and say it out loud)

Fill up on Jesus, and you will soon overflow with his fullness, and you will realize that you, too, are, "The disciple whom Jesus loved."

So I invite you to imagine yourself in the crowd of disciples and onlookers at each one of these encounters. Imagine you are sitting with Jesus when Nicodemus arrives that night. Or watching as Jesus and the Samaritan woman at the well go back and forth. Perhaps place yourself as that person to whom Jesus is talking.

Listen for his tone. Watch for his smile. Look into his eyes. Put yourself into each encounter, and you will walk away as they all did, changed forever.

JUST SO YOU UNDERSTAND MY METHODOLOGY:

1. I use the term "Family of Followers" as opposed to "church," because the word church is not found in the Bible. And certainly the early Family of Followers, typically gathering in their homes, were anything but what "church" looks like today.

2. I capitalize the Way, as well as Brothers and Sisters, to set them apart from our ordinary use. The Way is Jesus' Way, and the Brothers and Sisters are born again Christians.

3. You will notice I shy away from using "Christian" because that term has lost all meaning.

4. I also capitalize "Self" because I want to draw your attention to what a monster your Self is.

5. I use the apostle Paul's Hebrew name, Saul, predominantly, because John would have most likely called him by his Hebrew name, not his Greek name, Paul.

1

EYES BLAZING!

The hair on his head is white like wool, as white as snow, and his eyes are like a blazing fire! His feet are like bronze glowing in a furnace, and his voice is like the sound of rushing waters.

I am overwhelmed with an emotional tidal wave. I have been knocked to the ground by a blinding light. I cannot feel my body as I lay here prostrate, overwhelmed by a supernatural sense of this enormous … how might I say it? – energy!

Yes, that's it – an other-worldly kind of energy swirling all around me, and all over me – even through me. And weight. The air around me is heavy with a supernatural presence. It is his presence. His voice is overwhelming me. His eyes are almost blinding me. My body is shaking uncontrollably.

I am covered in rocky dust, in my eyes and ears, my hair, my nose. I cannot seem to open my eyes. The air is heavy, thick, and weighing down on me, pressing me into the dust. I feel like I have been blinded by the Light. I have just collapsed onto this rocky ground, so typical of this exiled island of Patmos. It is not as if I just fell down. No, it is more like my legs just gave out. My body folded in the presence of such a sight, of such enormous energy.

The sun is incredibly bright in the sky, but he is even brighter.

It is him. Jesus. My Lord, my Savior, my dearest friend. Yet it is not him. At least not the Jesus who walked and talked with us each day as we followed him throughout Galilee and Judea. This Jesus, this supernatural Jesus before me now, is the same God-Jesus we witnessed on the Mount of Transfiguration.

This is the Jesus I wish you all could see and experience, in this life, at least just once. One glimpse of this Jesus and all your seemingly overwhelming problems would diminish to mere fleabites. One glimpse of this Jesus, his hair on fire and his eyes like blazing torches, and your preoccupation with yourself, and your troubles, would simply disappear.

But I am getting ahead of myself.

I, John, your brother and companion in the suffering and kingdom and patient endurance that are ours in Jesus, was on the island of Patmos because of the word of God, and the testimony of Jesus. On the Lord's Day I was in the Spirit, and I heard behind me a loud voice like a trumpet, which said: "Write on a scroll what you see and send it to the seven churches: to Ephesus, Smyrna, Pergamum, Thyatira, Sardis, Philadelphia and Laodicea."

I turned around to see the voice that was speaking to me. And when I turned I saw seven golden lampstands, and among the lampstands was someone like a son of man, dressed in a robe reaching down to his feet and with a golden sash around his chest.

Yes, it is Jesus, but not like I knew him all those years ago. In his right hand he held seven stars, and coming out of his mouth was a sharp, double-edged sword. His face was like the sun shining in all its brilliance. When I saw him, I fell at his feet as though dead.

And, by the way, so would you. It is almost amusing to me when I hear people say something like, "The first thing I am going to do when I get to Heaven is ask God …."

My friend, that is the one thing you will not do. The one thing you will not be able to do. The one thing you will have no desire to do. There will be nothing casual, nothing ordinary about any such encounter. You will not be asking questions. You will not be quizzing God Almighty, El Shaddai! And even more so, you can rest assured there will be no need to ask anything. In that moment all your questions will either melt away or they will be answered.

You will see Jesus as I am seeing him now. And you will fall on your knees, as Isaiah prophesied,

> "As surely as I live," says the Lord, "every knee will bow before me;" every tongue will acknowledge God.'"

Trust me on this. You will either be collapsing on your knees in abject fear or kneeling in wonder and worship and adoration. Any encounter with Jesus, God Almighty, will leave you forever changed.

I am prostrate on the ground, energy and power and light swirling all around me. Am I afraid? Yes, and no. Yes, but no. It is not a frightened fear. Instead, the best I can describe it is an overwhelming feeling of power, and of being overpowered. A sudden sense of, "I am nothing and you are everything," kind of fear.

Awe and reverence. With an emphasis on awe. Reverence and respect. With an emphasis on reverence. Later, as I ran through this in my mind, contemplating it over and over, I concluded this is what the psalmist meant when he said,

> The fear of the LORD is the beginning of wisdom,
> and the knowledge of the Holy One is insight.

DEEP CALLING DEEP

But then Jesus placed his right hand on me and said: "Do not be afraid, John. I am the First and the Last. I am the Living One; I was dead, and now look, I am alive forever and ever! And I hold the keys of death and Hades."

Jesus was looking into my very heart. I felt a stirring in my soul. There was some kind of communication going on, but not with words. It was deep calling unto deep.

I think Psalm 42 captures it best:

> Deep calls to deep
> in the roar of your waterfalls;
> all your waves and breakers
> have swept over me.

In the "roar of the waterfalls" of his voice his touch was so familiar. His steady hand calmed me, just as it had done so many times before. I stood up, shook the dust off me, and looked at him, Jesus, bright shining as the sun, as glorious as a Sabbath morning overlooking the Sea of Galilee from the top of Mt Arbel. And in the midst of this whirling energy and power, my heart suddenly ached for our days back when we spent so much time together. All the times we laughed together. His kind eyes. His joyous laughter. His steady hand. Walking across our beautiful Galilee together. Out on the Lake of Gennesaret.

I prefer to call the Sea of Galilee, Gennesaret because this is our Hebrew word for harp. Yes, the lake is shaped like a harp. But even more so, after my time with Jesus, and whenever I think about our time on the lake, the word harp just feels appropriate.

Perhaps it is the sweet melody of the lake I love so much. The lapping of the gentle waves, the sea birds calling out to one another. The breeze ruffling the shoreline trees. Or maybe a harp reminds me of Jesus and the sweet melody of his words.

I think back to our last time with Jesus on the lake. We had been fishing all night but had caught nothing. Jesus called to us from the beach and beckoned us to come have breakfast with him. (I will tell you more about our miraculous catch later.)

The fire was crackling and giving off a comforting warmth in the coolness of the early morning chill on the sandy shore of the lake. The smell of fresh fish filled the air as a light breeze moved across us. Beside me was Jesus. We had been seeing him off and on for the past few weeks, since his resurrection. We never knew when he would appear, but when he did, my heart would leap for joy.

It was like old times with Jesus. He seemed to so enjoy this kind of quiet, even lazy gathering of friends. So many, many times, we laughed together, teasing one another about some blunder we had committed. Jesus would laugh and tease us as well. He was so much fun to be with. I miss him so much.

I was momentarily lost in my reverie. But then Jesus brought me back to the present by declaring,

> "Write, therefore, what you have seen, what is now and what will take place later. The mystery of the seven stars that you saw in my right hand and of the seven golden lampstands is this: The seven stars are the angels of the seven churches, and the seven lampstands are the seven churches."

While he was speaking, even though the sound was like a roaring river in full crest, I could sense his other voice speaking into my heart. The deeper voice I heard so many times over those three-plus years we were together. Deep calling unto deep. His calming, reassuring, loving voice. And I was suddenly swept back to that momentous day on the beach when he called us out of our fishing boats to follow him.

BOYS ON THE BEACH

Young John Mark wrote down what Simon Peter had to say about that fateful day. (John Mark became Peter's scribe, and I still call him young John Mark, even though so many years have passed.) Here is how he described it:

> As Jesus walked beside the Sea of Galilee, he saw Simon and his brother Andrew casting a net into the lake, for they were fishermen. "Come, follow me," Jesus said, "and I will send you out to fish for people." At once they left their nets and followed him.
>
> When he had gone a little farther, he saw James son of Zebedee and his brother John in a boat, preparing their nets. Without delay he called them, and they left their father Zebedee in the boat with the hired men and followed him.

As we know, Simon Peter is not one for excessive words, so allow me to add a little more detail to this account. You see, we had all met Jesus long before that day. Andrew and I met him first while following John the Baptizer. We would from time to time slip away from the strenuous and oft-times boring labor of fishing. Neither my big brother, James, nor Andrew's big brother, Simon, liked us doing this. Simon Peter especially would growl displeasure under his breath when we would return, and just as often, not even under his breath.

"Well, the return of the lazy boys!" he bellowed on one such occasion. "We were wondering if either of you had any backbone left for some actual work. Are you here to fish, or will you be drifting off again to follow, who is it you're following around these days, that crazy desert prophet, John the Baptizer?"

Peter and James were separating the fish they had caught that night and mending their nets. My father's workers were assisting them.

My big brother would just as often join Simon in berating us, but at other times he would step in and defend me. I loved that about James. He was tough on me, but he also loved me and was always looking out for me. So, on that particular day James stepped out of his boat and glared at Simon, saying, "Simon, you big oaf, you look after your own little brother, and I will look after mine."

My guess is James was already irritated with Simon that morning, as he sometimes was. This was most likely due to Simon trying to boss him around while they were out fishing that night. Simon could be bossy, and although James would often just ignore him, I guess today was not one of those times. Andrew, who was rarely intimidated by his big brother, blustery as Simon could be at times, smiled and said, "Yes, as a matter of fact we were with John, and he was baptizing near the Jordan."

Andrew paused, and then grinned and looked at his big brother and said, "You know, Simon, you don't have to work *all the time*. You could use a little time with the prophet, too. It might do you some good. Maybe polish off some of those rough edges!"

James roared with laughter, bending over and almost choking from his glee. Simon of course retorted with something like, "Work all the time? I wish I could get you two lazy boys to work just some of the time!"

It was a typical day on the beach. Big brothers and little brothers. So often laughing together, and just as often fussing with each other. I loved those days together. The sun glistening off the water like scales on a fish. The air so fresh, just breathing it was like a tonic for the soul. A gentle breeze was wafting across the air. Life was so simple back then. We just did a day's work and felt satisfied.

We thought we were happy, and I guess we were. But there was no real joy in our hearts. No pervasive sense of well-being. And the peace that passes all understanding? The peace that only Jesus can give, not as the world gives, was not even a fleeting thought. You see, back then we did not know what we did not know.

JOHN THE BAPTIZER

On that particular day Andrew and I had news for our big brothers. We had been with John the Baptizer as he immersed people in the Jordan, near Bethany in Judea. But a new man had walked onto the scene. His name was Jesus. This new man was different. This Jesus had an unusual, calm, relaxed pace. He was completely self-assured, confident even, yet there was nothing prideful about him. He was clearly comfortable with himself, and so very much at peace. He just had an air about him. An aura that captured your attention and drew you to him the moment your eyes connected with his.

And if his eyes connected with yours, it was as if he was looking straight into your soul.

We had all traveled up to Jerusalem from Galilee for one of our annual Jewish feasts. While we were there Andrew and I had slipped away to spend a couple of days with John. He was a wild sight, that is for sure. But you knew you were in the presence of holiness the moment you encountered him. Not man holiness; God holiness. John was a prophet, about that there could be no argument.

John's clothes were made of camel's hair, and he had a leather belt around his waist. He ate locusts and wild honey. People went out to him from Jerusalem and all Judea, and the whole region of the Jordan. Confessing their sins, they were baptized by him in the Jordan River.

The Jewish leaders in Jerusalem sent priests and Levites to ask John to explain who he was. But when he saw the Pharisees and Sadducees coming to where he was baptizing, he said to them:

> "You brood of vipers! Who warned you to flee from the coming wrath? Produce fruit in keeping with repentance. And do not think you can say to yourselves, 'We have Abraham as our father.' I tell you that out of these stones God can raise up children for Abraham. The ax is already at the root of the trees, and every tree that does not produce good fruit will be cut down and thrown into the fire."

For a moment John glared at the Jerusalem entourage, and then he continued,

> "I baptize you with water for repentance. But after me comes one who is more powerful than I, whose sandals I am not worthy to carry. He will baptize you with the Holy Spirit and fire."

John was not the type to mince words. Before they could ask him any more questions, knowing they might think he was posing as the Messiah, he confessed freely, "I am not the Messiah."

John knew what they wanted to ask before they uttered a word. You see, John knew he was a divinely appointed prophet. No doubt his mother Elizabeth had shared with him his miraculous birth – she was well past child-bearing age – and the prophecies foretold about him. And he also knew everyone was wondering if he was the long-awaited Messiah. Anticipation for the arrival of the Messiah was at a fever pitch all over Galilee and Judah. The prophecy from Daniel made it clear it could be any year, really any day now.

So these men from Jerusalem asked him, "Then who are you? Are you Elijah?"

He said, "I am not."

"Are you the Prophet Moses talked about in Deuteronomy?"

He answered flatly, "No."

Finally, utterly frustrated, they said, "Who are you? Give us an answer to take back to those who sent us. What do you say about yourself?"

I looked at Andrew, and we both waited to hear what John would say next. What would he say about himself? His next words surprised us, and you can be sure they stunned these Jerusalem priests and Pharisees because John presented himself as the one who would usher in the Messiah.

John replied in the words of Isaiah the prophet, "I am the voice of one calling in the wilderness, 'Make straight the way for the Lord.'"

I looked at Andrew and he looked at me, both of us a bit confused by the rhetoric bouncing back and forth between John and these men from Jerusalem. The Pharisees stepped forward and began to question him further. "Why then do you baptize if you are not the Messiah, nor Elijah, nor the Prophet?"

"I baptize with water," John replied, "but among you stands one you do not know. He is the one who comes after me, the straps of whose sandals I am not worthy to untie."

This was all happening at Bethany on the other side of the Jordan, where John was baptizing. (While Andrew and I were, as Simon would say, goofing around.)

2

WHAT DO YOU WANT?

Now what happened the next day changed our lives forever. I can look back on many momentous occasions in my three-plus years with the Master, but the genesis of them all was this quiet, almost surreal interaction we witnessed between our rabbi, John, and this new man, Jesus, who had suddenly appeared on the scene.

The next day John saw this man coming toward him and said,

> "Look, the Lamb of God, who takes away the sin of the world! This is the one I meant when I said, 'A man who comes after me has surpassed me because he was before me.' I myself did not know him, but the reason I came baptizing with water was that he might be revealed to Israel."

We knew right away John was saying this new man, Jesus, was the Messiah … the "Lamb of God who takes away the sin of the world." But had John lost his mind amid all his prophetical ranting? Could this man actually be the Messiah – the long-awaited Son of God? This man, this simple man standing in front of us? He was just a man. Not a king. Certainly not the Savior of Israel; he did not look like someone who would overthrow the despised Roman yoke.

We thought the Messiah would be a conquering king, much like our King David. A warrior king. He would free us from the oppression of Rome, just as Judas Maccabeus, who defeated the Greeks and liberated Israel had done a century before. Judas was a true hero to our people. He led the Maccabean Revolt against the Seleucid Empire, the remaining fragment of Alexander the Great's empire.

Judas' "army" was comprised of Jewish dissidents, and they defeated the Seleucid dynasty using guerrilla warfare tactics. His example of bravery and victory inspired hope in our people that we could do the same against the Romans. We had defeated the Greeks; why couldn't we defeat the Romans?

But most of us realized it would have to be the long-anticipated Messiah to defeat such a vast and terrifying Roman army. But when he did, Israel would be a proud independent nation once again, just as we were under King David. But this man did not look the part. And this 'Lamb of God' talk conjures up images of a sacrificial lamb, not a conquering king.

We obviously had missed Isaiah's prophecy about the "suffering servant." I will include a few excerpts, but you must read the entire passage, as it is astounding that so many of us missed this aspect of our "conquering Messiah:"

> Who has believed our message
> and to whom has the arm of the Lord been revealed?
> He grew up before him like a tender shoot,
> and like a root out of dry ground.
> He had no beauty or majesty to attract us to him,
> nothing in his appearance that we should desire him.
> He was despised and rejected by mankind,
> a man of suffering, and familiar with pain.

Like one from whom people hide their faces
he was despised, and we held him in low esteem.

But he was pierced for our transgressions,
he was crushed for our iniquities;
the punishment that brought us peace was on him,
and by his wounds we are healed.

We all, like sheep, have gone astray,
each of us has turned to our own way;
and the Lord has laid on him
the iniquity of us all.

He was oppressed and afflicted,
yet he did not open his mouth;
he was led like a lamb to the slaughter,
and as a sheep before its shearers is silent,
so he did not open his mouth.

I wanted to ask John to explain what he meant by, "A man who comes after me has surpassed me because he was before me," but John was not the type to suffer too many questions, so I kept my thoughts to myself. But Andrew and I talked about it all night and were determined to get some answers the next day from either John or this new man, Jesus.

John had apparently baptized Jesus previously, although we did not know exactly when. But our friend Matthew later described it like this:

> Then Jesus came from Galilee to the Jordan to be baptized by John. But John tried to deter Jesus, saying, "I need to be baptized by you, and do you come to me?"

> Jesus replied, "Let it be so now; it is proper for us to do this to fulfill all righteousness." Then John consented.
>
> As soon as Jesus was baptized, he went up out of the water. At that moment heaven was opened, and he saw the Spirit of God descending like a dove and alighting on him. And a voice from heaven said, "This is my Son, whom I love; with him I am well pleased."

The next day, as Andrew and I wondered about this man who so captivated our own captivating rabbi, John turned and looked directly at us. His eyes were intense as he gave this testimony:

> "I saw the Spirit come down from heaven as a dove and remain on him. I myself did not know him, but the one who sent me to baptize with water told me, 'The man on whom you see the Spirit come down and remain is the one who will baptize with the Holy Spirit.' I have seen and I testify that this is God's Chosen One."

When we heard him say this, we could not help but want to pursue this new rabbi. We were drawn to him. It was as if we were swept along with him. The sheer force of his presence, although understated, was irresistible. My feet were moving before I had time to even ask rabbi John if he approved of us following Jesus.

Andrew was already walking ahead of me. He told me later, "John, it was like a supernatural force was drawing me towards Jesus. I knew I should have asked our rabbi if we could leave him to follow this 'Lamb of God,' but there was no time for that."

As we followed Jesus closely, keeping a few steps behind, and not yet understanding why we were following him, he suddenly turned, looked at us, and asked, "What do you want?"

With that question my life changed forever. "What do you want?"

JESUS PLUS

May I pause in my story and ask you to think about his question?

If Jesus were to stand before you today, even as we speak, and ask you this same question, how would you answer him? It was not uncommon for Jesus to ask this when someone approached him for help. Rest assured he was never asking for his own information. He wanted the other person to think about why they were approaching him. Were they just looking for relief from a problem, or perhaps a blessing of some kind, or did they even know what they wanted from him? Most importantly, Jesus wanted them to think about whether they wanted *him*, or just what he could do for them.

How would you answer Jesus if he asked you? What is it you truly want from him?

Over the years I have observed three general answers to Jesus' question, this question he ultimately asks each of us:

1. We want his help and/or his blessings
2. We want Jesus Plus
3. We want Just Jesus

Let me explain.

Help: What we often want is just some help, or a blessing of some sort. All we are looking for is for Jesus to fix something, or so often someone. Whatever it is, whoever it is, we want things to be different. Or better. We want Jesus to fix / change / improve / or just make it, or them, go away.

We think that by being good, or at least acting better, or perhaps if we are a bit more religious, we can move Jesus to move for us. We want him on our side, but we are not ready to side with him. What we want is for Jesus to do something for us, but certainly not *in* us. At this point in our spiritual journey Jesus is impersonal. He is a positive source, hopefully an asset, but little more. In fact, this defines our spiritual life at this stage: a little religious, but not very personal.

We want his help, but we do not really want him.

Jesus Plus: If we are growing at all in our spiritual journey we have now moved from an impersonal, religious Jesus, to a personal *association* with Jesus. But all too often we still think it is Jesus-plus, as in we want Jesus, yes, but the plus is whatever we think we must have to be happy. We have come to realize we need Jesus for happiness, but we also need the plus. Be it more money, more material goods, more success, more children, a better spouse, what have you, we realize Jesus is important, but so is the plus. Perhaps the plus is even more important than Jesus, although we would never say that.

We want Jesus in our lives, but we do not truly believe he is enough. We need the plus.

At this stage in our spiritual journey we want a more personal *association,* but not really a personal relationship, because that kind of relationship may require too much of a commitment. We want Jesus to invest in us, and what we want, but we are not ready to invest in him. We only want to borrow from him.

Neither of these first two stages will ever bring us the "Life to the full" Jesus wants for us.

Thankfully, I have long since journeyed to this third stage: Just Jesus. And it has made all the difference. The difference between an empty life, and the life that is truly life, about which Jesus so often talked and taught.

Just Jesus: At this point in our journey we want Jesus and just Jesus. All else, though it may be nice, is not necessary. I want to share with you a short story to illustrate my point. When my father, Zebedee, died, he left a small bag of coins for our family servant, Mariam, who had been a part of our family for years. She had raised us from the time I was a child and was still helping Mother out at the time my father died. Both my mother and Mariam were grieving Dad's loss heavily at the time.

When my mother gave the bag of coins to Mariam, she looked at the coins inside, I am sure more money than she had ever received at one time, pondered them for a moment, and then quietly uttered this: "I'd rather have him."

The money Abba left for Mariam would be helpful, and no doubt she appreciated it so much. But in the end, she would trade his money for him without blinking an eye.

Inheritance is something we leave for someone. Legacy is something we leave in someone.

"I'd rather have him."

And so would I.

I would rather have Jesus as my Lord and my Savior, and my best friend, and an ever-deepening relationship with him, than all the possessions in the world. I would rather have just Jesus, than have my problems fixed. Oh sure, I enjoy nice things, and I would like my problems fixed. But I want nothing that might get in the way of the true richness of knowing Jesus personally, intimately.

Paul said it like this in his letter to the church in Philippi:

> But whatever were gains to me I now consider loss for the sake of Christ. What is more, I consider everything a loss because of the surpassing worth of knowing Christ Jesus my Lord, for whose sake I have lost all things.
>
> I consider them garbage, that I may gain Christ and be found in him, not having a righteousness of my own that comes from the law, but that which is through faith in Christ—the righteousness that comes from God on the basis of faith.

> I want to know Christ—yes, to know the power of his resurrection and participation in his sufferings, becoming like him in his death, and so, somehow, attaining to the resurrection from the dead.

That, my friend, is where I hope you are. Or that you will now make it your every desire to seek him with all your heart.

"I'd rather have him."

I just want Jesus. I know he will do good things for me. I know he will enhance my life beyond anything I could ask for, or even imagine asking for. But I do not spend any energy on those things anymore, because I just want him.

Because truly, "In him is life, and that life is the light of the world."

I have learned not to pray for more things, or even for relief from some negative situation, although it is fine to lift up our concerns to Jesus and our Heavenly Father. But for me, I just don't have the need to ask for anything. I know he knows what I need. I know he loves me perfectly. And I know he is aware of all the details of my life.

So I just ask for more of him.

Jesus has promised us if we seek him, truly seek just *him*, and not Jesus-plus, he will take care of all those other things – in just the right way. Actually, in just the perfect way.

I remember so clearly Jesus teaching us,

> "So do not worry, saying, 'What shall we eat?' or 'What shall we drink?' or 'What shall we wear?' For the pagans run after all these things, and your heavenly Father knows that you need them. But seek first Jesus, and all these things will be given to you as well."

So, my friend, the next time you approach Jesus for help, ask yourself first, do I really know what I want? Do I even really know him? Who is it I am approaching? Is it an impersonal, fix-it God, or my very personal, best friend … and my Lord and Savior?

3

MEETING JESUS

Now back to that day by the Jordan River. When Jesus turned and asked us, "What do you want?" we were completely taken aback. We were not prepared for such a penetrating question. I was so befuddled by his mere presence I could not form any words. His eyes were so piercing, and yet so peaceful. Piercing and peaceful. Is that possible? Yes, that might be the only way to capture the way Jesus looked at you.

One thing is for sure, he knew our thoughts before we did. Jesus could see right through the eyes in our head and directly into the eyes of our heart.

Andrew stumbled out the dumbest answer one could imagine, “Rabbi” (which means “Teacher”), “where are you staying?”

I have kidded him many times over the years for such a silly reply. He takes it well, but often responds, “Well, someone had to say something, John. You were just standing there with your mouth open and your tongue tied! I did the best I could.”

Jesus, in his calm, relaxed manner, simply smiled and replied, “Come, and you will see.”

So we went and saw where he was staying, and we spent that day with him. It was about four in the afternoon. The next day the first thing Andrew did was to find his brother Simon and tell him, “We have found the Messiah” (that is, the Christ).

Of course Simon Peter was skeptical and waved Andrew off. “I have no time for chasing after all these prophets, little brother.

If I did as you do, we would all starve. And besides, if he is so great, I am sure I will meet him sometime."

But this time Andrew would not take no for an answer. He was undaunted. He badgered Simon, even promising to work extra if he would just come and see. Finally, Simon agreed, I'm sure just to get Andrew to stop pestering him.

As we approached Jesus he was sitting in the shade. It was a hot day, but as we approached a breeze suddenly stirred. Was it the Spirit? Jesus stood and looked at Simon. For a moment he regarded him. Then he said, "You are Simon, son of Jonah. You will be called Cephas."

"You are Simon, son of Jonah. You will be called Cephas" (which, when translated is Petros … Peter). Jesus was giving Simon a nickname, Rocky, one that would prove most appropriate in our ensuing discipleship years.

It is hard to say what Simon was thinking, but he could not stop looking into Jesus' eyes. Later, he told me he could feel the earth shifting a bit under him. He could feel Jesus' eyes in his very soul. He said he had no idea what was coming next, but somehow, he knew Jesus was not going away.

A few weeks after Andrew and I met Jesus, we had another encounter with him, and this is the one that began our new life with him. It was like an earthquake, rattling the very core of our lives. Nothing would ever be the same again. After this day everything changed for all of us. And now, all these decades later, I can still remember the sights and sounds, the smells and the emotions of that day.

I shared with you earlier John Mark's somewhat abbreviated account of that day we "dropped our nets and followed Jesus." Remember, John Mark wrote his story of our time with Jesus from the many times he listened to Simon Peter talk about our three-plus years together. Now I will fill you in on the rest of the story.

It was several months later. We were near Capernaum, on the upper end of Lake Gennesaret (Galilee), at the Seven Springs, our favorite place to finish a night of fishing and to wash out our nets. This spot is called Tabgha and is well known by most fishermen, because the springs gushing into the lake make it a perfect place to wash our linen nets.

This is how Doctor Luke describes this momentous day:

> One day as Jesus was standing by the Lake of Gennesaret, the people were crowding around him and listening to the word of God. He saw at the water's edge two boats, left there by the fishermen, who were washing their nets. He got into one of the boats, the one belonging to Simon, and asked him to put out a little from shore. Then he sat down and taught the people from the boat.
>
> When he had finished speaking, he said to Simon, "Put out into deep water, and let down the nets for a catch."
>
> Simon answered, "Master, we've worked hard all night and haven't caught anything. But because you say so, I will let down the nets."

Now please understand Simon was not being deferential to Jesus. He was not being obedient. He was tired. He was hungry. He was irritated. We all were. Our hard night of fishing had been a waste of time. Simon was in no mood for some itinerant rabbi to tell him how to fish. He rolled his eyes and said sarcastically, "But because *you* say so (*rabbi – who knows so much about fishing*), I will let down the nets."

Jesus knew he was being sarcastic. Jesus always knew what we were thinking – and he knows what you are thinking, too. So please learn, as we did, to be transparent with him. You are not fooling him when you are trying to be extra religious, or really spiritual, so as to garner some favor from him. And there is no need to try to hide your dark thoughts from him either.

He knows all, and he loves all, as well. With Jesus, there is now no condemnation. Conviction, yes, but no condemnation. He convicts our hearts, telling us we can do better, but he never condemns us. One of my favorite stories, which I will tell you in greater detail later, is when we were at the temple one morning and Jesus was teaching. Suddenly a group of angry Pharisees came storming up and practically threw a young woman to the ground in front of Jesus. She had been caught in adultery. When the dust settled and the mob had dispersed, Jesus gently but firmly said to the young woman, "I do not condemn you. But," and here follows his conviction, "You can do better, so stop living this way."

Conviction but no condemnation.

Jesus knew Simon was being sarcastic, and he still loved him, not despite his usual stiff-necked self, but because of it. Jesus also knew what he had planned for Simon. Since the day Andrew had first introduced Simon to Jesus, Simon had tried to ignore this captivating rabbi. When we would invite Simon to come spend time with Jesus, his response would be to scrunch up his face and snort something, mostly unintelligible. No words, just snorts.

Simon, like so many people, was trying to ignore that pull in his heart, that pull drawing him to Jesus. He tried to stay busy, he tried to stay away from Jesus. He was trying anything and everything to keep his life as he had so carefully designed it. That pull inside his heart was telling him Jesus would change him, and he was afraid of letting go and surrendering.

Jesus knew all this, and that day on the shoreline he was going to get Simon's attention, and in a big way. Dr. Luke continues the story:

> When they had done so, they caught such a large number of fish that their nets began to break. So they signaled their partners (that would be James and me) in the other boat to come and help them, and they

> came and filled both boats so full that they began to sink.
>
> When Simon Peter saw this, he fell at Jesus' knees and said, "Go away from me, Lord; I am a sinful man!" For he and all his companions were astonished at the catch of fish they had taken, and so were James and John, the sons of Zebedee, Simon's partners.

As Simon kneeled before Jesus, exasperated, and exhausted, there was a moment, a hesitation, a look between the two of them. I saw it and felt a stirring in my own soul. There was some kind of communication going on between them, but not with words. It was deep calling unto deep.

Then Jesus said to Simon,

> "Don't be afraid; from now on you will fish for people."

So we pulled our boats up on shore, left everything and followed him. All of us: me, big brother James, Andrew, and Simon. Simon Peter was cut to the heart that day, and his reaction was like so many others before him, who have experienced an up-close and personal encounter with Jesus.

Isaiah cried out,

> "Woe is me! I am ruined! For I am a man of unclean lips, and my eyes have seen the King, The LORD Almighty."

Job confessed,

> "My ears had heard of you
> but now my eyes have seen you.
> Therefore I despise myself
> and repent in dust and ashes."

For the first time Simon saw Jesus for who he is, and therefore who he himself was – a sin-filled, weak and selfish sinner - and the result was a heart cut to the core. This is the way of any true encounter with the Master. My friend, if you have not had this experience, I wonder if you have truly come face to face with the risen Lord?

4

COVERED IN THE DUST OF THE RABBI

Then Jesus said to Simon, "Don't be afraid; from now on you will fish for people." So they pulled their boats up on shore, left everything and followed him.

You may think it irresponsible of us to drop our nets and follow this itinerant rabbi. You may even be surprised that even our big brothers, James and Simon, always so serious and focused on work, followed, too. What about our father? Were we deserting him? Did he feel abandoned?

Quite the opposite. You see, in our world, the ultimate dream of any Jewish father is for his son to become a rabbi. Short of that, it would be to be included as a rabbi's disciple. In our culture it is the pinnacle of life. And as you will see, this Jesus was quickly understood to be a "Rabbi with authority." To be a disciple of a rabbi with authority, like Jesus, is more than anyone could ever hope for.

Was our father, Zebedee, disappointed when we dropped our nets to follow Jesus? I can tell you it was one of the happiest days of his life. He was thrilled. His boys were with the rabbi Jesus, whose renown was already spreading throughout Galilee. I think Abba may have done a back-flip off his boat!

Growing up as Jewish boys, our history is taught from the Torah and the Prophets, not Greek or Roman or world history. Every Jewish boy wanted to be a rabbi. It was to be the best of the best. The most admired. The most respected. And of course, one would be serving Yahweh, the ultimate desire for any Jewish man.

Are you interested in how our education as children progressed? For our first five years our parents train us at home. Starting at around age three they begin to expose us to the Torah. The first thing we learn is the Shema. The *Shema* - "Hear, O Israel" - are the first two words of a section of the Torah that is the centerpiece of our morning and evening prayers, every day of our lives. Jesus said the Shema every day, morning and evening, as we all did.

From age five to twelve or thirteen, we study each day at our Beth Sefer. This means 'House of the Book.' If the village is big enough to have a synagogue, the Beth Sefer is held in an attached room. In Jerusalem only boys attended, but in Galilee both boys and girls were included. Our local rabbi would be our teacher.

During this time in our education, we memorize and study the Torah, and we learn how to ask good questions. This is the Jewish way, and especially the rabbi's way. It is said if you have three rabbis in a room, you will have five opinions! Jesus was a master at asking questions. You will notice that when he is approached and asked a question, he typically answered with a question.

For instance, you may recall the story of the Torah expert approaching Jesus:

> On one occasion an expert in the law stood up to test Jesus. "Teacher," he asked, "what must I do to inherit eternal life?"

Jesus answered in good rabbinic fashion, by asking a question in return:

> "What is written in the Law?" he replied. "How do you read it?"

Jesus' mother, Mary, told Dr. Luke about the time the family traveled up to Jerusalem for the Feast of Passover, as they did every year. Jesus was twelve years old, and already adept at asking questions. He had good training from his father, Joseph, as well as at his Beth Sefer in Nazareth. On the return trip Mary and Joseph lost track of Jesus, each assuming Jesus was traveling with the other, either in the men's group or the women's group. At age twelve he could have been in either.

When they discovered Jesus was not with either traveling group, they hurried back to Jerusalem, terrified of what may have become of their son. But where do they find the young, not yet discovered Messiah? In the temple - asking questions, of course. Dr. Luke again gives us the story:

> After three days they found him in the temple courts, sitting among the teachers, listening to them, *and asking them questions*. Everyone who heard him was amazed at his understanding and his answers. When his parents saw him, they were astonished. His mother said to him, "Son, why have you treated us like this? Your father and I have been anxiously searching for you."
>
> "Why were you searching for me?" he asked. "Didn't you know I had to be in my Father's house?"

Mary told us she made a little game out of Jesus' training to be a rabbi. When he would return home from school, instead of asking, "What did you learn today?", she would ask, "Did you ask any good questions today?"

Now at the conclusion of Beth Sefer, the boys and girls have reached twelve or thirteen years old, and the girls are off to get married. Most of the boys go to work as an apprentice with their fathers, learning the family trade. This is when James and I joined our father's fishing business. We were good students, but only the best move on to study further.

Our father would have been thrilled if we had been selected to continue with our education, studying and memorizing the Torah completely, as well as the Law and the Prophets, and even the Oral Torah. This is the next step in the education of a rabbi-to-be, the Beth Midrash.

Beth Midrash is only for the best and the brightest. Soon the young man is following a rabbi. He becomes a Talmid, a disciple, along with his Talmidim, his fellow disciples. To become a disciple, the young man must approach a rabbi and present himself, asking the rabbi if he can be his disciple. If the rabbi finds the young man suitable, he says to him, "Come, follow me."

I CHOSE YOU

This is exactly what Jesus said to us: "Come, follow me." But please do not miss the fact that *we* did not approach Jesus and ask to be his Talmidim, he approached us. This never happens in the Jewish rabbinic world. The would-be disciple always approaches the rabbi. On our last night with Jesus he reminded us of this:

> "You did not choose me, but I chose you and appointed you so that you might go and bear fruit—fruit that will last."

Yes, he chose us, because he had a purpose and a plan for us. I am so grateful he did. He sought us out. Even though we were not on the rabbi/disciple tract, he saw something in each of us. He had a plan for our lives, and it was far beyond anything we could have imagined. As a matter of fact, if we had imagined even a fraction of what he had in store for us, I am sure we would have never dropped our nets to follow him.

I, for one, probably would not have even gotten out of my boat!

He has a plan for your life, as well. You do know this, I hope. And even as you are reading this, he is seeking you, calling you. You are not an accident, not just a product of nature. You are his fine craftsmanship, created in Christ Jesus to do good works which he has planned in advance for you to do.

Never lose sight of this. You are not ordinary in the Master's eyes. You are, you absolutely are, his fine craftsmanship. And he is seeking you. You know it. You feel it. Please do not ignore his call. Open up to it. Receive it. He will do all the rest.

The relationship between a Talmid and his rabbi is much more than teacher-student; it is more like a father-son relationship. The rabbis taught: "If you must choose between saving your father or saving your rabbi, save your rabbi first. Because although your father brought you into this world, your rabbi brings you into the world to come."

A Jewish phrase describes this close relationship this way: A disciple is to be "Covered in the dust of the Rabbi," because we are following so closely. It is indeed a fine thing to be covered in the dust of Jesus.

If a rabbi agreed to allow a young man to become his disciple, the disciple understood he was to totally submit to the rabbi's authority. Not just in his teaching and his interpretation of the scriptures – what we call the rabbi's yoke – but in all areas of his life. He wanted to emulate his rabbi in the way he lived, even in the way he ate, drank, and slept. In essence, in every detail of his rabbi's life.

THE DISCIPLE JESUS LOVED

Our fishing ended, and our lives began when Jesus said to Simon, "Don't be afraid; from now on you will fish for people."

So we pulled our boats up on shore, left everything and followed him.

Yes, we did. We followed him. For the next three-plus years we followed him to weddings, to funerals, to feasts and to famines - famines of the soul, that is. We followed him through glorious praise and through violent criticism. And never once did he flinch from his purpose. He was driven, he was compelled, he was undaunted, and yet he did everything with his typical calm, relaxed pace.

How might I describe my time with him? Perhaps I can best sum it up in one word: love. God is love. Whoever lives in love lives in God, and God in them. This is how love is made complete among us so that we will have confidence on the day of judgment: In this world we are like Jesus. There is no fear in love. But perfect love drives out fear, because fear has to do with punishment. The one who fears is not made perfect in love.

This, my dear child, is why I am called, "The disciple whom Jesus loved." Not because I think he loved me more than the others. Jesus was not capable of something as human as unequal love. He loved all equally. No, I call myself this because this is the lasting, indelible impression he left in my heart. He loved me.

The disciple that Jesus loved was not the disciple Jesus loved the most, he was the disciple who lived the rest of his days fueled the most by his love.

Through all the good times and bad, through the miracles, the parables, the teaching and the training, the overarching, compelling message I felt, what we all felt, was his enduring love. Yes, he would at times be frustrated with our lack of faith. Yes, at times he would press us and challenge us as to why we were so slow to understand him and his mission. But through it all, he loved us.

And now we love, because he first loved us.

I want you to know he loves you just as much as he loved us. My hope is that as you read this story you will come to see yourself - yes you - as "The disciple whom Jesus loved."

When you begin to see yourself as the disciple whom Jesus loved, his joy and his peace and his freedom will become more and more a part of your life. All of these will guard your hearts and your minds in Christ Jesus. He will guard your heart against the attacks of the accuser, the adversary, Satan, because he wants to create doubt in your mind. Doubt that Jesus actually loves you. Doubt that he cares about the details in your life. Doubt that he even likes you.

"How could he love you, knowing everything about you, as he does?" Satan whispers in your ear. "You are a phony, a fake Christian. If others only knew the real you! Jesus does know, and there is no way he could love you, and he certainly could not like you."

But those are all lies. Yes, he does know every weakness, every sin, every fear and even every hypocritical thing you have ever said and done. And he was still willing to die for you. Because you too can be the disciple whom Jesus loved.

5

MARY'S STORY

Yes, I am John, son of my father, Zebedee, son of my dear mother, Salome, and younger brother to James. I am compelled to tell you my story. No, it is not my story I want to tell, but the story of our three-plus years with Jesus. It is therefore Jesus' story I want to tell you. I want you to know Jesus as we did. I want you to experience his friendship as we did. You may be thinking this is not possible.

You may be thinking that because we had such intimate, one on one, personal experiences with him, we had, and now still have special access to him. Or you may be thinking that this kind of friendship is no longer possible because Jesus is no longer walking this earth physically.

You would be wrong on all counts.

In my years since Jesus ascended back to the Father, I have grown closer to him than during the times we walked together. Why? Because we still walk together. He has not left me. He is not away, somewhere, watching me from a distance. He is right here with me. I feel his presence as real as when we stood side by side on those dusty roads in Galilee.

Quite frankly, I would not be surprised in the least if at any moment he appeared out of the air around me. He is that close. To me, yes, but to you as well. Please know that. Please receive that into your heart. He did this many times after his resurrection. For forty days he would just appear, seemingly out of thin air. But of course, the air is never thin when one is walking with Jesus. It is always thick with his presence.

With each resurrection appearance he was demonstrating to us that he was indeed in the air all around us. He wanted us to know we were always in his Kingdom. He wanted us to always feel his presence, to know that at any moment he could just appear right beside us. I live this way now. I know he is with me. This is why I talk with him and walk with him daily. He wanted us to live this way, so he purposely appeared and reappeared over those forty days after his resurrection, proving to us his constant presence.

I still see his smile. I feel his warmth. His mischievous eyes still bedazzle me. His sense of humor still lifts my spirits. His calm, relaxed pace still settles my anxiety. His strength still strengthens me.

I am not alone in this intimate relationship with Jesus. Many of his followers, who never knew him while he was here on earth, have the same deep relationship. You can, too. You know this, I hope. Yet I wonder if you do. This is why I am compelled to write our story.

You see, John Mark, Matthew, and Luke have provided us with excellent accounts of Jesus' life. You would do well to spend time studying their accounts. Mark was in Rome when he wrote his account. His story was gleaned from the many stories he heard directly from Simon Peter, while he was preaching, teaching, and oftentimes just telling stories among friends and fellow followers.

Matthew was in Antioch, Syria when he wrote his account, and his intended audience was our fellow Jews. You will see this with all his references to our Hebrew Bible prophecies. If you pay close attention, you will see he is comparing Jesus to Moses – as in a new Moses, come to deliver his people from the bondage of slavery. Only this "Moses," this Jesus, came to deliver us from a different kind of slavery – our slavery to our Self.

Dr. Luke wrote his account for a specific benefactor, Theophilus. Theophilus was Greek, so you will notice Dr. Luke addresses whole-world issues more so than Jewish issues. The kind of issues the Greeks were always studying and debating. But Luke certainly intended for his gospel to also speak to the Jews, along with the entire Greco-Roman world. He started his letter to Theophilus this way:

> Many have undertaken to draw up an account of the things that have been fulfilled among us, just as they were handed down to us by those who from the first were eyewitnesses and servants of the word. With this in mind, since I myself have carefully investigated everything from the beginning, I too decided to write an orderly account for you, most excellent Theophilus, so that you may know the certainty of the things you have been taught.

"So that you may know the certainty of the things you have been taught." This is quintessential Dr. Luke. He was so precise. He rooted his account in history, with dates, and rulers identified. He interviewed most of these eyewitnesses and disciples of Jesus while Paul was in prison in Caesarea Maritima, up on the Mediterranean coast. The city King Herod the Great built.

My heart warms each time I read Dr. Luke's words about his conversation with Jesus' mother, Mary. In his gospel account he related Mary's own words to him, as she told him about the birth of Jesus and his early years. Twice he wrote what Mary had said to him:

> But Mary treasured up all these things and pondered them in her heart.

I was there with Mary for this discussion. Dr. Luke had taken the opportunity to travel around and interview all the eyewitnesses while Paul was imprisoned at Caesarea for those two years. He came to Jerusalem to see Mary first.

I sat with Mary and Dr. Luke as she pondered the wonder that was the birth story of her baby, Jesus. I was with her because Jesus asked me to take care of his mother. As Jesus hung on that horrible cross, nearing death, Mary had walked over to him - stumbled over is more accurate. It was gut-wrenching to watch his dear mother mourning and suffering over her precious son. I will spare you the details because truly it is just too hard for me to relive that experience.

But I knew Jesus' death was near, so I walked over to stand by Mary's side, as her heart broke in agony for her son. In that moment Jesus looked down at us and said, in halting words, gasping between breaths,

> "Woman, here is your son." And to me he said, "Here is your mother."

From that time on I took Mary into my home. She and my mother Salome were relatives and dear friends. We stayed in Jerusalem for the next thirty years. As the family of followers grew, Mary helped us with her cooking and taking care of the needs of the various families. She was such an asset during those early days. But her biggest contribution to the new Way was just her presence.

Can you imagine what an encouragement it was to have the mother of our Savior right there with us? Oh, how many times did I watch as new converts, both Jews and Gentiles, would gather around Mary, many sitting at her feet, their eyes wide as saucers, as she retold tales of Jesus' youth.

Her warmth and her steady, loving presence were priceless and precious. I miss her even to this day. Mary died a quiet, dignified death in Jerusalem. She lived to see her son's new Way expanding across the known world. She lived to see rich and poor, slaves and freedmen, men, women and children, Jew and

Gentile, all surrendering their lives to the Savior of the world. Her son.

Then Mary breathed her last and died at a good old age, an old woman and full of years; and she was gathered to her people.

EPHESUS

After her death I moved to Ephesus, the crown jewel of Asia. Saul, better known these days as the Apostle Paul, had spent three years there and established a strong and thriving community of Followers of the Way. But sadly, Paul had been executed by that madman Nero, the emperor of Rome. As had Simon Peter. Thirty years have passed since that time, and I still miss them both, especially Peter.

Simon and I had a unique, special bonding experience together while we were with Jesus. And our relationship went even deeper during the early years of the Way. I wish you could see the two of us together back then. A more opposite pair of friends there could not be. Simon Peter, with his blustery, bombastic self. He was much bigger than I, and stronger, and older.

But I was no wilting wallflower, as some have mistakenly thought. I was young, but I could hold my own with Simon. After all, it was James and me, you will recall, who wanted to call down fire on that Samaritan village. But together, and with the Holy Spirit, we made a perfect, imperfect pair. We laughed together, we cried together, and we sometimes argued together. But through it all we grew closer and closer.

He could finish my sentences, and I his. But I am getting ahead of myself, as I am wont to do. I will share more later about my dear friend Simon, and the Apostle Paul, as I tell this story.

I have lived in Ephesus since I moved here from Jerusalem, and I know I will breathe my last here. The Lord has shown me this. I spent two years in exile on Patmos because I refused to worship the emperor Domitian. He was calling himself God. Actually, he called himself the Savior of the World and the Son of

God. (Does this sound familiar?) It was his fourteenth year as emperor, and he had handed down an edict that everyone was to worship him and offer sacrifices to him.

I refused to do so.

A temple to Domitian had been built in Ephesus a few years prior. This temple is huge, about the size of Domitian's ego. It was there we were ordered to offer these sacrifices and worship him. I flatly refused to do so. My refusal, as well as my teaching and preaching the Gospel of Jesus Christ, the true Savior of the world, the true Son of God, eventually reached Domitian in Rome, and I was packed off to Patmos.

Domitian was a despotic ruler, cruel and spiteful and hateful, and the people of Rome eventually assassinated him. After his death they scratched his name off all public monuments to him. I was subsequently freed and returned to Ephesus. It is from here I am writing to you.

This crown jewel of Asia is a magnificent city. Outside of Rome it is one of the most important cities in the empire, with a population of 250,000. This is a very sophisticated city with a theater that seats 24,000, a stadium and a temple to Artemis, whom the Romans call Diana. This temple is simply magnificent. It has 127 columns and is four times the size of the great Parthenon in Athens.

As I mentioned before, Paul spent three years here teaching and training a group of young men to carry forward the message. Through the years, nine apostles and evangelists spent important time in this most important city. My dear brother Simon Peter ministered here. Our faithful friends, Priscilla and Aquila, helped Paul establish the first community of Followers here, before returning to Rome, only to return back to Ephesus again, as Nero's wild persecution of the Christians grew out of control.

This is my home now. My adopted home. Jerusalem is no more. Ransacked and burned to the ground by the Romans. I will be put to rest here in Ephesus. But Galilee will always be my true home. The rolling hills, so green and inviting, and the waters of the Jordan River and the Sea of Galilee will always be in my blood. Of course, my true home still awaits me. I know I will go there soon.

Luke began his account of the life of Jesus like this, "I, too, decided to write an orderly account for you, most excellent Theophilus, so that you may know the certainty of the things you have been taught."

ENCOUNTERS ALONG THE WAY

Here is how I will start mine:

This is the testimony: God has given us eternal life, and this life is in his Son. Whoever has the Son has life; whoever does not have the Son of God does not have life.

I write these things to you who believe in the name of the Son of God so that you may know that you have eternal life.

I want you to know the Jesus I knew. Mark, Matthew and Dr. Luke have done excellent jobs with their accounts. I wish not to add to their stories, but to enhance the theme and thrust of Jesus' life and ministry. His earthly ministry, that is. He is still fully engaged in our lives in his heavenly ministry, through the presence and the indwelling of his Holy Spirit.

Mark, Matthew and Dr. Luke did well in including parables, teachings and various miracles. You can trust their stories. I was an eyewitness to them. They are completely accurate. I have no need to repeat their stories, or even the parables, or Jesus' teachings, as wonderful as they are. I want you to meet Jesus, yes, actually meet him personally.

It became obvious from the start Jesus wanted us to know his Father as he knew him: a loving, gracious, compassionate and forgiving Heavenly Father. Jesus knew we, the Jews, did not know him in this way. Now, as I write these words to you, I am compelled by the same desire: I want you to know Jesus, as we knew him. As we know him even now. And it is obvious that too many do not, in fact, know him at all.

So we are going to sit in together on a select few encounters Jesus had with various people during our years together. Encounters with wise men, and down and out women. With physically blind men and men who were spiritually blind. Encounters with everyday men and women, just like you and me, as well as encounters with governors and kings. We will sit in on their conversations because conversations bring us into the heart of the matter. Conversations reveal so much. My desire is that through these encounters you will encounter the real Jesus.

The first three Gospel accounts give us the history of Jesus. I want to explore the mystery of Jesus. The first three accounts give us the heart of Jesus, but I want you to feel the heartbeat of Jesus.

We will watch as Jesus drills straight into the hearts of these men and women. It was simply amazing to witness Jesus boring directly into their souls and shining his Light into the depths of their being. He immediately understood the deep essence of everyone he met. No one was going to fool Jesus. And although he was a wonderful friend, and so much fun to be around, when it came to these God-ordained encounters, he wasted no time drawing the man or woman into the Light.

Together we will feel their fears, listen to their questions, and share in their newfound joy. Or frown with sadness as we watch them walk away, as blind as before.

You see, no one is ever the same after an encounter with Jesus. He always brings us to a defining moment. A crisis of the will. Jesus presents us with a crossroad, a choice. A choice to either follow him through the narrow gate and into eternal life, or to reject him, and be swept along the broad road that leads to destruction.

His exact words were,

> "Enter through the narrow gate. For wide is the gate and broad is the road that leads to destruction, and many enter through it. But small is the gate and

> narrow the road that leads to life, and only a few find it."

But he leaves the choice with us. Sometimes I wish he would not. I wish he would force us to follow him. But this is not the way of the Master. If we will only receive him, surrender to him; if we will only embrace his offer of his life to the full, he will inevitably and absolutely bump the trajectory of our life. And nothing will ever be the same again.

It never is, after one experiences the true presence of the Master.

6

IN THE BEGINNING

Where to begin with the rest of this story? I am an old man now. My end is near. But while I still have life and breath in me, I press on to take hold of that for which Christ Jesus took hold of me.

I think it is appropriate to begin our journey together at the beginning. Because …

> In the beginning was the Word, and the Word was with God, and the Word was God. He was with God in the beginning.
>
> In him was life, and that life was the light of all mankind. The light shines in the darkness, and the darkness has not understood it, nor overcome it.
>
> There was a man who was sent from God, his name was John. He came as a witness to testify concerning that light, Jesus, so that through him all might believe. He himself was not the light; he came only as a witness to the light.
>
> The true light that gives light to everyone was coming into the world.
>
> He was in the world, and though the world was made through him, the world did not recognize him. He came to that which was his own, but his own did not receive him. Yet to all who did receive him, to

> those who believed in his name, he gave the right to become children of God— children born not of natural descent, nor of human decision or a husband's will, but born of God.
>
> The Word became flesh and made his dwelling among us. We have seen his glory, the glory of the one and only Son, who came from the Father, full of grace and truth.
>
> Out of his fullness we have all received grace on top of the grace already given. For the Torah was given through Moses; grace and truth came through Jesus Christ. No one has ever seen God, but God the one and only, who is at the Father's side, has made him known to us.

I am eager to continue with you through our entire story with Jesus, but I have a reason for these things I am writing. Let me explain why I have chosen these words so carefully. If you have read my Gospel, these words are familiar to you. But sometimes familiarity breeds unfamiliarity. So, if it pleases you, I will pause to expound briefly on my "prologue" above. Because these words matter.

One interesting note before we dive into the prologue. You will see that I use LORD and Yahweh interchangeably. They are in fact the same word in our Hebrew scriptures. When you see LORD that is just the Greco-Roman, Gentile word for Yahweh.

I want you to notice that "In the beginning, *God* created the heavens and the earth." We see the name "God" used throughout the first seven days of creation:

> And God said, "Let there be light,"
> And God said, "Let there be a vault between the waters …"
> And God said, "Let the water under the sky …"
> Then God said, "Let the land …"

But when the focus becomes the story of man, we see the name "LORD God" is introduced for the first:

> This is the account of the heavens and the earth when they were created, when the LORD God made the earth and the heavens.

Our Hebrew word for God is Elohim. We see this name in our very first verse. Elohim is the creator God – and by the way, it is plural, showing us the triune nature of God right away! Elohim is not necessarily an impersonal God, but LORD ... Yahweh ... is the very personal, relational name God gives himself. So when the Holy Spirit is telling us about creation, he uses Elohim. But when the story becomes about God's relationship with man, his very personal relationship with man, the Holy Spirit introduces God's personal, intimate, relational name: "LORD God."

LOGOS AND LIGHT

I live in a Greco-Roman world these days. Ephesus is as Greek and Roman a city as there is in the Roman empire. Behind Rome, and along with Alexandria, and Antioch, Ephesus is one of the most important cities in the empire. We are inundated with Greek philosophy, as well as Roman culture.

This is why I am starting my story with, "In the beginning was the Word ... (the Logos), and the Word ... (the Logos) was with God, and the Word, (the Logos) was God.

This concept of Logos has been around for centuries. To the Jews, Logos means the Word of God, the expression of God - his principle of divine reason and creative order. To the Greeks, Logos carries with it a sense of Universal Meaning. The principle that orders the world. Reason. Supreme Logic. The highest principle of cosmic order.

As you can see, the Jews and the Greeks both see Logos as supreme reason and logic and the source of meaning. But we

Jews understand this through the perspective of God Almighty. As smart as they are, the Greeks are not really sure what they understand.

Heraclitus was a well-known early Greek philosopher. He lived six hundred years before Jesus. He was famous for his musings about the meaning behind the universe. He contemplated the fact that nature and everything in our world seems to be in constant change. As he famously stated, "No man can step in the same river twice. For he is not the same man, and it is not the same river."

(This is the kind of navel-gazing that drove my can-do, always-active friend Simon Peter to distraction. I wish you could see his eyes rolling whenever he was around this kind of talk.)

With the world in a constant state of change, Heraclitus finally concluded there must be a Logos, a Word or reason of God, with a purpose and design to the world and world events.

Plato then came along a couple of hundred years later and said this,

> "It may be that someday there will come forth from God a Word, a Logos, that will reveal all mysteries and make everything plain."

Plato's statement may surprise you, coming from such a famous Greek philosopher, but Plato was a monotheist. He did not worship Yahweh, but he was not fooled by the multitude of gods the Greeks and Romans worshipped. He knew there had to be just one true God. He just did not know *the* one true God.

As you can see, this idea of Logos has been around for a long time. And why not? Everyone knows there is a God, they just do not know the God who is the only true God. But what may be known about God is plain to everyone, because God has made it plain to everyone. For since the creation of the world God's invisible qualities—his eternal power and divine nature—have been clearly seen, being understood from what has been made, so that people are without excuse.

The problem for the Greeks and the Romans, as well as so many others even today, is that although they knew there had to be a God, they neither glorified him as God nor gave thanks to him, but their thinking became futile, and their foolish hearts were darkened. Although they claimed to be wise – all these famous Greek philosophers, governors, kings and such - they became fools and exchanged the glory of the immortal God for images made to look like mortal human beings and birds and animals and reptiles.

This is what one sees all around Ephesus, and all over the Roman empire. The Greco-Roman world is a very "religious" world. Everyone is a polytheist. Gods are everywhere. Household gods. Mythical gods. All of them are just silly, make-believe gods, representing anything and everything one can imagine.

But are you ready for an interesting twist to this story about the Logos? Heraclitus, the first to expound on this concept of Logos, lived here in Ephesus – right here where I am writing to you. Ironic, yes?

The beginning of all this contemplating and philosophizing about the Logos began here in Ephesus. From Ephesus it traveled to Athens, the world-famous center of learning, knowledge and philosophy. All the Athenians and the foreigners who lived there spent their time doing nothing but talking about and listening to the latest ideas such as this.

But the true Logos, the actual Logos, became a real man; a real man born in the little town of Bethlehem. He came of age in Galilee. His life was spent inside Israel, a backwater outpost in the minds of these sophisticates in Athens and Rome. But now we have brought the true story of the Logos here to the crown jewel of Asia.

> In the beginning was the Logos, and the Logos was with God, and the Logos was God.

I wish I could say to Heraclitus and to Plato, "You have been speculating about this Logos for all these centuries, and now I am here to tell you it has come. The Logos has come. But it is not an "it" - it is a man. It – he – is the Son of God. His name is Jesus."

We have seen him. That which was from the beginning, which we have heard, which we have seen with our eyes, which we have looked at and our hands have touched—this we proclaim concerning the Word of life. Yes, the life appeared; we have seen it and testify to it, and we proclaim to you the eternal life, which was with the Father and has appeared to us.

And my friend, you who are reading this and those who will read this someday, the message we are proclaiming to the world, we proclaim to you, too. We proclaim what we have seen and heard, so that you also may have fellowship with us. And our fellowship is with the Father and with his Son, Jesus Christ. We write this to make our joy complete.

Yes, I am sharing this story, my story, but yet truly his story, with you, so that my joy will be complete. There is nothing that compares to the joy of seeing someone find Jesus, surrender their life to him, and begin to live Jesus' life to the full. So, I will continue to write, and to proclaim the Son, so that my joy becomes your joy, and thus will be complete.

7

RECEIVE

Jesus came to that which was his own, but his own did not receive him.

Yes, Jesus is the light of the world, but we all - each of us - must receive his Light, and then his Life within us will follow. We receive it as a gift. We do nothing to earn it, that is for sure. To help illustrate this, I want you to pause for a moment and think about this idea of receiving a gift.

I am purposely using the Greek word 'paralambano' for 'receive.' Perhaps my Greek-speaking friends fully understand its meaning, but my Hebrew friends might well miss it.

Paralambano means 'to take with' or 'to join oneself to.' This is what receiving this gift of Life looks like: we join ourselves to the giver, Jesus. We receive the Holy Spirit with us, within us, and take him into our hearts.

As an example, think about this: what if I gave you a gift, and you took it but never opened the package. Did you *receive* this gift?

What if I gave you a gift, and you opened it, but then set it aside, rarely, or even never using it, or even looking at it again. Did you receive my gift? Of course not. So please understand what I am saying. For you to become a child of God, you must "join yourself to Jesus," embracing him and absorbing him, and living with the knowledge and understanding of his heart-felt love with which the gift was offered.

As Paul wrote,

> You must take hold of *that* - this gift of Life - for which Christ Jesus took hold of you.

This is what *receiving* the gift of eternal life looks like. When Jesus appeared to me on the Isle of Patmos, he compared receiving him to opening the door to our hearts to him:

> "Here I am! I stand at the door and knock. If anyone hears my voice and opens the door, I will come in and eat with that person, and they with me."

This is just one of the many things so wonderful about Jesus. He is always standing at the door of your heart. He does not want to give up on you. He stands unwavering; he even knocks. You have heard his knock, haven't you – deep in your soul? His gentle, but persistent knock?

He loves you, so please open that door and receive him. And, if you have already opened that door, open it even wider. That is in part what "taking hold of that for which Christ Jesus took hold of me" means. Open the door. Fling it open – wide open! Take hold of the gift. Make it yours. Receive it. Make it real in your life.

CHILDREN OF GOD?

Once, when we foolishly tried to move a few little children away from Jesus so he could interact with the adults around us, Jesus noticed and was indignant. He said to us, with that stern glare only he could pull off,

> "Let the little children come to me, and do not hinder them, for the kingdom of God belongs to such as these. Truly I tell you, anyone who will not *receive* the kingdom of God like a little child will never enter it."

We receive his gift as a child opens and receives a gift. But this is too difficult for many prideful grown-ups. They bristle at the idea of being like a little child, and many bristle at the idea of simply receiving a gift. They want to earn it. They want to own it. But we simply cannot earn anything from Jesus.

It is his gift of grace: unmerited favor. Not merited, not earned; only given, to be received.

> Yet to all who did receive him, to those who believed in his name, he gave the right to become children of God - children born not of natural descent nor of human decision or a husband's will but born of God.

"... he gave the right to become children of God": This statement may shock you, this idea that everyone is not born a child of God. Yes, he loves you; you are his dear creation. But no, you are not born a child of God. You must become a child of God. You must be reborn into his family. We will explore more on this idea of being born again when we get to Jesus' conversation with Nicodemus, but for now let me remind you of what John the Baptizer said to the Jewish authorities when they approached him, as he baptized near the Jordan River:

> "And do not think you can say to yourselves, 'We have Abraham as our father.' I tell you that out of these stones God can raise up children for Abraham."

John was warning them not to assume they were part of God's family just because they were born in the lineage and nationality of Abraham. This is what I am writing today to you, too:

children born not of natural descent,
nor of human decision
or a husband's will,
but born of God.

Too many people mistakenly think that because they are children born of natural descent, to parents who are Christians, or they made an intellectual or practical decision to follow Jesus, or from a husband's will, that their salvation is secure with God.

Please hear me on this: You are not born a Christian. You must be *reborn* a Christian. And we do not "make a decision for Christ." No, you fall on your knees and surrender to him. You fall on your knees and surrender to him as your Savior. As *the* Savior, the only one who can possibly rescue you from your Self – and from your sins. And to be blunt, from Hell.

You receive him like a child. No grown-up decisions. Only child-like surrenders. You open the door to your heart and receive his Light and his Life. Your parents cannot do it for you. Your rabbi or your preacher cannot do it for you. I certainly cannot do it for you.

You, my friend, must receive his grace.

"He gave the right to become children of God."

Don't miss: "to *become*." You see, all of us who were the first Christians were born Jews: God's chosen people. And since the Jews were God's chosen people, quite naturally we just assumed salvation was our birthright. How could it not be?

Already today, I see in the children of the Followers of the Way, the second and third generation, just assuming that because their parents are Christians, so are they.

But our first birth, our natural physical birth, means absolutely nothing. If we want to think in terms of a birth, then Jesus is saying, "There must be two births: The first by water through your mother's womb, and the second through the Spirit." Yes, we are not born into his family: we *become* children of God.

JESUS MOVED IN WITH US

> *The Word became flesh and made his dwelling among us. We have seen his glory, the glory of the one and only Son, who came from the Father, full of grace and truth.*

The Logo became flesh and made his dwelling – *his tent … his tabernacle* - among us.

When God the Father directed Moses to set up a tabernacle in the wilderness, the purpose was so that the people could come to the tabernacle to be with God. This was true for the temple, as well. The temple in Jerusalem was simply the tabernacle, but now as a building, instead of a tent.

When Jesus came, he was the temple incarnate. God, in the form of the Son, came to be with us. We no longer have to go to a temple to be with God. Jesus walked and talked with us.

When Jesus returned to Heaven, he sent the Holy Spirit. The Holy Spirit is now the temple, but this temple is in us. Did you get that? The temple is now in us. This is the mystery that no one previously understood – not the scholars, the religious elite, and certainly not the Jewish people. Brother Paul put it succinctly in his letter to the Colossians:

> the mystery that has been kept hidden for ages and generations, but is now disclosed to the Lord's people. To them God has chosen to make known among the Gentiles the glorious riches of this mystery, which is Christ *in you*, the hope of glory.

As well as in his first letter to the Corinthians

> Do you not know that your bodies are temples of the Holy Spirit, who is in you, whom you have received from God? You are not your own; you were bought at a price.

Let me sum it all up for us:

Originally, we went to the temple *to be with* God.

God, in the nature of Jesus, then came *to be with us.*

Now we have the Holy Spirit, who indwells us, so we are now the temple. No more *with,* but now *in*!

So now, as Paul told the navel-gazers in Athens, "In him we live and move and have our being."

8

COME & SEE

John 1

Let's get moving with our "travel narrative." You recall that John the Baptist had just pointed Jesus out to Andrew and me at the Jordan River. We then started walking after him. Jesus turned around and asked us, "What do you want?"

He wasn't asking for information; he was asking so we would think deeply about what it was we did want. The first example of this was after Adam and Eve had eaten the fruit and were now hiding in the bushes. God the Father asked them, "Where are you?" He wasn't asking for information. He wanted them to think deeply about where they now found themselves after doubting his character. This is what Satan was successful in doing: getting Adam and Eve to doubt the goodness of God's character and his plan for their lives.

Jesus turned and asked us, "What do you want?" Neither one of us was ready for his question, so with perhaps the all-time dumbest answer ever, we fumbled out a lame, "Rabbi where are you staying?" Now in all the ways Jesus could have answered us, including something sarcastic like, "Is that the best you can come up with?" – he simply replied, "Come, and you will see."

This was so typical of the Master. Just a simple, "Come and see." The next day Jesus decided to leave for Galilee. So we followed him back home. When we arrived he found Philip, and said, in essence, the same thing to him: "Follow me."

We make things so complicated, don't we? We get into discussions and debates and even arguments about details that serve only to distract us from what is most important: following Jesus.

"Just come, follow me, and you will see."

Notice in Jesus' invitation to both Andrew and me, as well as to Philip, Jesus did not say, "Come sit over here and start taking notes about rabbinic theology." He did not say, "I have a five-point lecture on forgiveness, and following that a class on tithing, and following that we will discuss at length the meaning of Jonah and the whale, as well as Elijah and the widow in Nain."

He simply said, "Follow me ... (and as you do you will see and understand all that I have for you.)"

Now you may be thinking, "Okay, but you, John, literally followed a real man named Jesus. You walked around with him, learning directly from him. But what would that look like now, in my world?"

It looks like keeping your eyes focused on Jesus, first and foremost, especially when distractions and complications become clouding and confusing. Focusing on his presence with you, as well as his perfect love. It looks like following Jesus first, not following me first, or any of the other apostles, not your preacher, teacher, or church. Or any of the schisms that threaten to harm Jesus' Way.

It certainly looks like *not* following the culture around you – I hope that is a given. The culture is like a white-water rapid, the Jordan River in the rainy season, rushing around us, pulling us along with such a rapid and busy pace we miss what is most important. Remember again Jesus' words:

> "Enter through the narrow gate. For wide is the gate and broad is the road that leads to destruction, and many enter through it. But small is the gate and narrow the road that leads to life, and only a few find it."

The culture is that wide gate and broad road. Jesus is the narrow gate. Keep your eyes fixed on him. Throw off everything that hinders, and the sin that so easily entangles, and run with perseverance the race marked out for you.

For me following Jesus looks like slowing down and sitting with my best friend. Perhaps, simply by reading and contemplating his words. Yes, it can be just as simple as reading Jesus' words. I am constantly reading the whole of the scriptures, and yes, all scripture is God-breathed, inspired, and of absolutely equal importance. But there are times when reading just Jesus' words can be so comforting, and so clarifying. The fog lifts and the way becomes clear. When I lose my way, or the way is uncertain, I simply slow down, and follow Jesus, as he says,

> "I am the way and the truth and the life ... Follow me."

THE WAY OUT

I am reminded of a story a missionary named Tychicus shared with me just a few years ago. It seems he was taking the message of Jesus to a remote area around the Mediterranean. He was traveling with a guide as they sought to find an isolated village in the dense forest.

The guide got word from one of his fellow guides that there was a group of islanders who were hostile to the Christian Way and were trying to find them to do them harm. So the guide changed course and took my friend deeper into the forest. After the guide had waited a sufficient time for the danger to move away from them, he motioned for my friend to gather his things, to resume their hike.

My friend Tychicus told me he looked all around him and all he could see was dense forest. There were no paths, and as far as he could tell there was no way to get back to the path on which they had been traveling. Frustrated, and a little fearful, Tychicus looked at the guide and said, "We are lost and surrounded by thick, dense trees and bushes. How are we going to find a way out of here?"

The guide looked at Tychicus for a moment, pulled his machete out, turned and started to hack away at the underbrush. Then he stopped, turned to my friend, and said, "Get behind me and follow me. I *am the way out*."

As is the Master. He is the way out. The way out of the culture. The way out of the prison in which we so often put ourselves. The way out and the way into the life to the full.

OUR PATH IS SO SIMPLE: YOU FOLLOW ME

May I share with you two principles dear to my heart?

1. For a disciple of Jesus, the simple path is, "Follow me."
2. For a disciple of Jesus, the simple invitation to others is, "Come and see."

When we are confused, or distracted, or harried and hurried, and not sure what being a "good Christian" looks like, a simple step is to slow down, and simply follow Jesus ... and his words, and his teachings.

But it does not always feel so simple, or easy to do, does it? The whitewater current of this culture so quickly and easily distracts us, and Satan is always looking to confuse us. Even Simon

Peter, my dear friend and the great apostle, had to be reminded – and lovingly rebuked – because he forgot this basic principle.

We were fishing in the Sea of Galilee, after Jesus' resurrection. It had been a while since he had appeared to us. We were home, so we decided to do what comes naturally to fishermen – fish.

I will have a lot more to say about this encounter later in our story, but for now, the lesson is that even we apostles can become distracted and lose track of following Jesus.

After Jesus had cooked breakfast for us that day, he took Simon Peter off for a walk. I followed along at a distance. As they walked Jesus told Peter three times that his primary focus was to take care of his followers: "Take care of my sheep." Three times. Yet when Peter sees me following, he immediately loses his focus, apparently forgets what Jesus had just said – said three times, mind you - and asks, "Lord, what about him?"

I think any normal person would have rolled their eyes and possibly even raised their voice and responded, "Peter, did I not just make it clear, three times, your mission, and your focus, is to feed my sheep?" But Jesus simply answered, "If I want him to remain alive until I return, what is that to you? You must follow me."

Jesus' response is meant for us all: "What is that to you? You must follow me."

We might say, Yes, Jesus, but what about all the religious hypocrites?

Jesus' response: "What is that to you? You must follow me."

Or, "Okay, but what about the seven days of creation? And how did all the animals fit in the ark?"

Again Jesus would say, "What is that to you? You must follow me?"

Or, "What about God's sovereignty versus free will?"

"What about baptism? What about Gentile circumcision?"

"What about all the bad things done in the name of religion?"

What about … What about … What about …? - You fill in your own blank, but the answer is the same:

"What is that to you? In time I may make those things clear to you or I may not. But you must follow me."

Our Invitation is So Simple: "Come & See"

Now, there are many people you know who are not following Jesus, and they have similar questions. For them, your simple invitation is, "Come and see."

"Just come and see; just come and meet Jesus."

My fellow apostle, Matthew the tax collector, recorded one of my favorite things Jesus said,

> "Come to me, all you who are weary and burdened, and I will give you rest. Take my yoke upon you and learn from me, for I am gentle and humble in heart, and you will find rest for your souls. For my yoke is easy and my burden is light."

"Come to me," Jesus says, "when you are stressed out or confused or distracted. Just come to me, when you feel like you have a burden you cannot bear." I witnessed Jesus' calm presence reduce the stress and anxiety immediately in many people. His presence and his companionship will do the same for you.

Remember, I am writing these things to you so that you also may have fellowship with us. And our fellowship is with the Father and with his Son, Jesus Christ, and I want you to have this same fellowship. You can! And when you learn this, and lean into and appropriate this into your life, your joy and my joy will be complete.

"Come and see."

This is what Philip said to Nathanael. Philip, like Andrew and Peter, was from the town of Bethsaida. Philip was so excited about meeting Jesus that the first thing he did was go and find Nathanael. When he found him he told him, "We have found the one Moses wrote about in the Law, and about whom the prophets also wrote—Jesus of Nazareth, the son of Joseph."

Nathanael responded sarcastically, "Nazareth! Can anything good come from there?" Nazareth did not have a bad reputation, so I think Nathanael's sarcasm stemmed more from the natural rivalry between the fishing villages in this area of Galilee than anything nefarious about Jesus' hometown.

"Come and see," Philip simply replied.

Please notice Philip could have tried to explain about this man Jesus; he could have tried to reason with Nathanael; he could have cajoled him, or even tried to guilt him into following him. But Philip simply said, "Come and see."

Perhaps you can take a lesson from Philip the next time you want someone to meet Jesus?

I have encountered many men and women who have objections, and some with sincere questions. I feel confident I can answer their questions – that is if they really want an answer. Many do not. Their questions are only a diversion.

But many do have sincere questions. I am confident in my ability to answer their questions, but I am even more confident that if they will "come and see" Jesus, two things will happen: As they get to know Jesus, they will like him. Really like him. Many, many people who were not at all like Jesus, liked Jesus.

And, they will be surprised when they realize how much he likes them. Truly likes them. As I keep reminding you, yes he loves you, but he really likes you, too. Not sure about that? Just come and see.

NATHANAEL

I was sitting with Jesus when he saw Nathanael approaching. We had found some shade and were just chatting about our families and what was going on in each of our lives. Does it surprise you that Jesus would engage in ordinary, seemingly mundane conversations with us? Perhaps you think he was always serious, and always teaching and challenging us.

But keep in mind he was - and still is - such a good friend. Yes, a friend. He enjoyed these times together, with no crowds, and no agenda. Often, during these times we did most of the talking, and Jesus just sat back and took it all in. Jokes and funny stories were always part of the conversation, as well as good-natured ribbing. I wish you could see Jesus laugh. What a wonderful, free-spirited laugh he had!

He was so much fun, and he enjoyed parties and festivities, so much so that those who were against him spread rumors he was a drunk and a glutton. Once, when talking about John the Baptizer, he had this to say:

> "For John came neither eating nor drinking, and they say, 'He has a demon.' The Son of Man came eating and drinking, and they say, 'Here is a glutton and a drunkard, a friend of tax collectors and sinners.'"

Jesus was neither a drunk nor a glutton, but he was indeed a friend to tax collectors and sinners. Jesus enjoyed good food, good wine and good fellowship. I suppose this is one of the endearing and enduring things I remember most about Jesus. He was so real. We could just be with him. And it was obvious he enjoyed just being with us, his friends.

We laughed so many times together. Jesus could be such a comedian. You may have read in the other gospel accounts of Jesus calling James and me, "Sons of Thunder?" I will tell you more about that later, but he would often get a big grin on his face when he would see us approaching. He would look around at the other disciples, make a show of backing up, and bellow out, "Watch out, here come the Sons of Thunder!"

Once, when he was teaching about not judging others, he picked up a big stick and held it up to his eye, moving it closer and then away, and then back and forth, saying,

> "Why do you look at the speck of sawdust in your brother's eye and pay no attention to the plank in your own eye?"

Even his nickname for Simon Peter, Simon the Rock … "Rocky," was a nickname he laughingly employed often.

We were laughing at something Andrew had just said about his big brother, Simon Peter, who provided many laughs for us, when we looked up and saw Nathanael approaching with Philip. Jesus stood up, and I could see his demeanor change from casual, to one of purpose. But he was still smiling as he said to Nathanael, "Here truly is an Israelite in whom there is no deceit."

"How do you know me?" Nathanael asked, with a puzzled look on his face.

Jesus answered, "I saw you while you were still under the fig tree before Philip called you."

There was a moment, a hesitation, a look between Jesus and Nathaniel. I saw it and felt a stirring in my soul. There was some kind of communication going on, but not with words. It was deep calling unto deep.

Then Nathanael's face lit up and he declared, "Rabbi, you are the Son of God; you are the king of Israel!"

I will never forget the look on Jesus' face and his matter-of-fact tone as he replied,

> "You believe because I told you I saw you under the fig tree? You will see greater things than that." He then opened his arms, looked upward and said, "Very truly I tell you, you will see 'heaven open, and the angels of God ascending and descending on the Son of Man.'"

Nathanael's eyes were as big as saucers. Jesus had a huge smile on his face. He was not admonishing Nathanael, but he was clearly enjoying himself. Later, when I asked him if he was referring to Jacob's experience out in the wilderness, recorded in our Hebrew book of Genesis, he nodded, but then turned to me and said, "You boys are in for a real ride. If you think my seeing Nathanael under a fig tree is a marvel, let's head over to Cana. I have a wedding to attend. And you are going to experience a whole new world, my young friend."

9

WATER TO WINE

John 2

After we arrived back in Galilee, Peter and my big brother James joined my father out on the lake to get back to fishing. But Andrew and I were too enthralled with Jesus to think about anything else, so we followed Jesus and Nathanael to a wedding that was taking place in Cana. Nathanael was from Cana, and Jesus' mother was very close with the wedding family there.

It was Tuesday, the third day of the week. The third day was often chosen as the wedding day because on the third day of creation God said, twice, "It is tov … good." Thus, the day was considered twice blessed. Tuesdays were also ideal for weddings because this gave guests time to get there after the Sabbath, and to spend a few days after, before the next Sabbath.

In our culture weddings can last several days. They are a joyous affair, with the bride's family providing a feast of food and wine for all the guests from their village. Close friends from the surrounding villages, like Mary, are invited as well. Nazareth was just a few miles away from Cana, so we joined Mary, who had been there a few days before we arrived, helping her friend, Abigail, the mother of the bride.

Everyone was laughing and having a good time. The mood was festive, the food was delicious and plentiful, and the wine was flowing. We were just getting to know Jesus, so it was fun to see him in such a relaxed, festive setting. Let me say it again, if you have any idea that because Jesus is the Son of God, and the Savior of the world, he is not a fun friend to be around, well, think again.

It was getting cooler as the hot sun settled on the horizon, and the laughter and conversations were getting louder and more joyous. I was settling in after having eaten my fill when I noticed the wine steward pull Mary aside and say something to her. His face was serious, and after he spoke to her, her demeanor suddenly changed.

While we were eating and drinking, laughing, and mixing it up with the others under a tent, Jesus' mother walked over to Jesus with a stern look on her face. We could see something was wrong, but what could it be? She was not the hostess, but she was very close to Abigail, the mother of the bride, and she had been helping out all day.

She motioned for Jesus to step away with her. Jesus paused and looked around at us, but then stood up and stretched his back and legs as he stepped just a few feet away. I strained to hear Mary, and I heard her whisper, "They have no more wine."

If you live here in Ephesus, or you are a Gentile from Greece or Rome, you would have some idea of what a social disaster this would be. But in our culture, with its emphasis on social hospitality and reciprocity, and shame and honor, running out of wine would be much more than just an embarrassing social blunder. It would bring shame on the bride and groom for the rest of their marriage.

They would be known as the couple who ran out of wine. You see, each wedding in a village such as Cana would be an act of social reciprocity. I come to your family wedding and you "prepare the fatted calf." Yes, you would go all out to feed and entertain my family, and when I have a wedding, I would do the same.

EXCELLENCE IN EXCESS

The social fabric of our nation is woven together with this culture of hospitality. You may recall that when the three angels visited Abraham, he said to them,

> "If I have found favor in your eyes, my lord, do not pass your servant by. Let a little water be brought, and then you may all wash your feet and rest under this tree. Let me get you something to eat, so you can be refreshed and then go on your way—now that you have come to your servant."
>
> "Very well," they answered, "do as you say."
>
> So Abraham hurried into the tent to Sarah. "Quick," he said, "get three seahs of the finest flour and knead it and bake some bread."
>
> Then he ran to the herd and selected a choice, tender calf and gave it to a servant, who hurried to prepare it. He then brought some curds and milk and the calf that had been prepared and set these before them. While they ate, he stood near them under a tree.

Three seahs would feed a small village, as would a choice, tender calf. Abraham is going all out for his guests, as is the custom in our culture of hospitality. This is excellence in excess, as we will see with Jesus in just a moment. To do less would be a dishonor to his guests and bring shame on Abraham and Sarah. And did you notice Abraham ran to the herd? Men almost never run in our culture.

To run out of wine would bring shame on the family, and especially the young married couple, for years to come. It should not be this way, but it is. For the rest of their marriage the couple would be known as the couple whose wedding celebration was marred by shame and dishonor.

To try to put this into perspective for my gentile friends, imagine you threw a wedding celebration, and unbeknownst to you the meat was spoiled. Half of your guests got sick, and one even died. This may sound like an extreme example, but in our culture the shame and dishonor would be similar.

Wedding feasts are always meant to be a joyous celebration, and wine is the personification of joy. Our prophet Amos gives us this prophecy:

> "The days are coming," declares the LORD,
> "New wine will drip from the mountains
> and flow from all the hills,
> and I will bring my people Israel back from exile.
> "They will rebuild the ruined cities and live in
> them.
> They will plant vineyards and drink their wine;
> they will make gardens and eat their fruit."

As you can see, to run out of wine is to run out of joy. This situation is not just an embarrassment, it is a potential disaster. There would be no source for more wine. The wine was out. That was it. No remedy. No hope. The family is in serious trouble, and they need … a miracle.

I was not sure why Mary came over to Jesus, or what expectations Mary had of him, and maybe she did not either. But she knew two facts: there was a problem, and Jesus could help. She may not have known exactly how he could help, but she went to him anyway. This is a valuable lesson for us, as well. We know we have a problem, but we do not know the solution, and we do not have the power to solve it. But we know – we do know – Jesus knows the best solution, and we know – we do know - he has the power to resolve it in just the right way.

Mary seemed to assume Jesus would respond with compassion to this looming crisis. Perhaps she was counting on the fact that Jesus had already begun his public ministry, albeit a quiet beginning. He had a little band of disciples. He had been publicly baptized by her aunt Elizabeth's prophet son, John. As I observed over the coming years, when Jesus was faced with desperation and lost hope, compassion welled up in him, and he responded to meet the need, and to restore hope to the hopeless.

He still does this, my child. I hope you know.

So we may come to him, too. With no solution in sight, with no power in ourselves to resolve the situation, just simple trust, that he knows, and he cares. I have to admit I was taken aback by Jesus' response to Mary. He looked at her and said, "Dear woman, why do you involve me? My hour has not yet come." His expression was without emotion, but his eyes had a curious look.

Now we could debate what Jesus meant by, "My hour has not yet come," but what happened next is much more important. In that moment I noticed a change in both Mary's and Jesus' demeanor. There was suddenly a twinkle in their eyes, as they connected on a level to which I was not privy.

There was a moment, a hesitation, a look between Jesus and his mother. I saw it and felt a stirring in my soul. There was some kind of communication going on, but not with words. It was deep calling unto deep.

DO WHATEVER HE TELLS YOU TO DO

The mood had suddenly shifted. What was downcast was now cheerful. There was a sparkle of hope in Mary's eyes as she turned to the servants who had followed her, and said, "Do whatever he tells you."

I love that about Mary. What a wonderful choice God the Father made when he selected Mary to be Jesus' mother. "Do whatever he tells you." No specifics, no worrying about what it was Jesus would do. No need to try to control the outcome. Just "Do whatever he tells you."

Most of us, when faced with such a felt need, would be tempted to tell Jesus exactly what we need for him to do. Wouldn't you? We would think we know the solution, so we would go to Jesus, perhaps in prayer, and as we are asking him for help, we are at the same time telling him precisely what help we need.

Not Mary. When the angel Gabriel informed her she would be impregnated by the Holy Spirit and give birth to the Messiah, she simply responded, "Let it be to me as you have said."

In essence, "Do whatever he tells you."

Nearby stood six stone water jars, the kind we used for ceremonial washing. Stone jars were used for this because they were sturdy and not porous. We would pour this water over our hands, not to wash with soap and water, but for a ceremonial cleansing. The water in those jars was to provide a ritual cleansing.

These ritual jars, which held normal well water, were about to be transformed into jars that held a miracle of a new Living Water. The jars each held from twenty to thirty gallons. I was now watching closely to see what Jesus would do next. He had stepped over to the jars and motioned to the servants to follow him.

The wedding festivities were still in full swing. Laughter and conversations were all around us. But within us was a quiet, wait-and-see feeling. My eyes were riveted on the Master. A sense of energy was moving around us like a swirling breeze. The wedding noise faded away.

Jesus then said to the servants, "Fill the jars with water." I was confused by this. Wouldn't you be? What is he going to do with six full jars of water? How would this solve the crisis at hand? The family needed more wine, not more water. But the servants began to get the water and fill the jars. This took some time, as they filled each of them to the brim.

As they were going about their tasks, Jesus kept looking back at us and smiling. I asked him what was happening, but he just smiled and whispered, "Wait and see."

When they had completed their task, Jesus told them, "Now draw some out and take it to the master of the banquet." I noticed right away the water was now red in color. And I was close enough to smell something different. Was it the smell of grapes? At this point I was totally captivated by this turn of events. Something had happened to that water, but exactly what, I was not sure.

The servants walked off with the new "water" and delivered it to the master of the banquet. I was watching him as the servants handed him the cup. He was a large man, and clearly a gregarious sort. He had been talking loudly with a couple of friends but stepped aside to take the cup. As he sipped the water that had turned into wine, his face lit up and a huge smile spread slowly across his face. He quickly drank the rest of the water-now-wine in one gulp.

He did not realize where it had come from, though the servants who had drawn the water did, and of course Mary and I knew. Then he called the bridegroom aside and motioned for everyone to be quiet. The chatting went on for a moment, but then he said with a loud voice, "Friends, I am astounded at the generosity and the hospitality of our hosts. Everyone brings out the choice wine first and then the cheaper wine after the guests have had too much to drink."

Several people laughed, and several looked around knowingly, nodding their heads, but the parents of the bride were clearly anxious. I do not think Mary had told them of the wine disaster, hoping I am sure to spare them from worry. But they were still nervous as to what the master might say next.

"Yes, everyone saves the cheaper wine for last, but you have saved the best till now!" He paused and wrapped his arm around the groom. "This is the best wine I have ever tasted!" he exclaimed, as he held the cup up. He motioned for the servants to start filling everyone's cups, and the music began again. The groom and the bride hugged and waved to everyone as they danced. It was such a wonderful time, and thankfully no one knew the disaster that had been averted.

Mary looked over to Jesus, then she winked at me, and re-joined the festivities.

10

ORDINARY TO SPECTACULAR

I have reflected many times on that first miracle Jesus performed in Cana of Galilee, and I now see it as a sign. It was the first of the signs through which he revealed his glory; and Nathanael, Andrew and I realized we each had a newfound trust in Jesus. The kind of trust that can only be imparted – not decided. I knew then I would follow this man, a man who apparently controlled nature, to the ends of the earth.

I thought about Moses turning the Nile's water into blood. That was surely a sign from God. But Jesus, he turned the water, not into blood, but into wine!

The words of our prophet Joel kept echoing in my mind:

> The threshing floors will be filled with grain;
> the vats will overflow with new wine and oil.

The water to wine was a sign through which Jesus revealed his glory. To glorify God is to *accurately reveal* him. This is precisely what Jesus was doing. He was giving us a picture of his Father: who he is, what he cares about, and how he does things.

After the wedding, on the walk back to Capernaum, we asked Jesus about the miracle we had just witnessed. He smiled and said, "I did that for three reasons, my young friends.

"First, for my dear mother."

"Second, for that young couple."

"And third," he hesitated, then looked each of us in the eye, and said, "for you."

At this he smiled at Nathanael and said, "I told you that if you thought my seeing you under the fig tree was something special, just wait. You will see a lot more than that." He winked at us and said, "I want you to know who I am, and who the Father is. I will teach you all this, but today I wanted to show you."

When you think of God what words come to mind? Are they positive, negative, or just kind of lukewarm? I think many people, especially those who have yet to meet Jesus and get to know him, would think of words like pedantic and petty, or boring, or judgmental. Perhaps confining, restricting, wrathful and condemning might also come to mind.

To them he is a 'bread and water God' - as in, "You are to be content with only bread and water, and that is all I promise to provide." Words associated with God such as fun and feasting, lavish, generous, happy and celebrating are foreign to them. Perhaps they would say his purpose was to run a tight ship, without a lot of fun being had, and his passion was, well, only aroused when he became angry.

They would be so wrong. So very wrong.

Jesus made two statements that define his purpose and his passion much more accurately than these misguided ideas:

> "And no one pours new wine into old wineskins. Otherwise, the wine will burst the skins, and both the wine and the wineskins will be ruined. No, they pour new wine into new wineskins."

> "Do not think that I have come to abolish the Law or the Prophets; I have not come to abolish them but to fulfill them."

Jesus is saying that he is bringing new wine, a new way of doing things. We will need a new heart to receive and fill up on this new wine. But he is also saying that he is not doing away with the old wine, the old way of doing things. Instead - and do not miss this - Jesus is *fulfilling* God's original purpose and passion. He is fulfilling the Mosaic Law, showing his Father's heart behind his teachings.

His purpose and his passion are for, "Streams of living water to flow from within us."

He is going to live out in vivid color the purpose of all the laws and commandments we find in our Hebrew scriptures. And because Jesus often gave us real-life demonstrations along with his teaching, his first miracle was to change ordinary water into spectacular wine.

Ordinary to spectacular.

No, he is no bread and water God. He is a God of feasts, celebrations, and lavish love. And he always has been. Our crusty Hebrew prophet, Isaiah, recorded God's own words about his purpose and passion:

> On this mountain the Lord Almighty will prepare a feast of rich food for all peoples, a banquet of aged wine - the best of meats and the finest of wines.

You have to love that, don't you? "A banquet of aged wine – the best of meats and the finest of wines."

When Mary came to Jesus with the wine problem, Jesus responded by taking six big jars of ordinary water and turning them into - are you ready? – over three thousand cups of the finest wine. Three thousand cups ... of "a banquet of aged wines – the finest of wines."

This is no bread and water God we serve.

Now to be sure there are times when bread and water are just the right thing for me. Jesus knows when I need just that, and so for a season my "feasts" may consist of bread and water. But later, when I have grown spiritually, and closer to Jesus, precisely because of that season of bread and water, I have always –

always – looked back and realized that season, too, was a lavish feast of his love. One that I needed so desperately, but just did not know it.

As we think about this first sign, I want to personalize this, and ask you to think about two things:

1. Where is your wine running out?
2. Where do you doubt … or cannot seem to trust or believe … or perhaps have lost hope … that Jesus will show up to produce the finest wine out of the ordinary water in your life?

WHO JESUS IS, IS WHO GOD IS

What Jesus did with this miracle tells us a lot about himself.

Over the years I have learned to ask three questions as I study our Hebrew stories.

What does this passage tell me about:

1. Who God is
2. What he cares about
3. How he does things

Jesus and God the Father are Social and Relational:

Jesus is at a wedding with his family and his friends. Stop and think about that for a moment. The Savior of the world, God Almighty, creator of the universe, is taking the time to … socialize.

Yes, Jesus is social and he is relational. He taught us efficiency can be the enemy of relationships. Efficiency has no time for deep relationships. He knew how important time with friends and family is to the overall body, mind and spirit. So he took the time. He was never in a hurry. Yes, he had a pace, but it was a calm, relaxed pace.

And I can assure you one of the reasons I call myself, "The disciple whom Jesus loved," is because relationships were so important to Jesus. One of my favorite images is that of God walking in the cool of the evening, as he visited with Adam and Eve. Isn't that a wonderful picture of our social, and relational Heavenly Father?

And so it is a wonderful picture of his son, as well.

WHAT JESUS CARES ABOUT

Jesus and God the Father are Caring and Compassionate:

Did you know the word 'compassionate' means 'to suffer with'? And therefore, to feel compassion for someone means "I can feel your pain in my heart." Jesus cares enough about this young married couple to be with them in their crisis, to feel the pain they would feel in their impending social suffering and humiliation.

So he acted with compassion.

My friend Simon Peter wrote this in his first letter:

> Humble yourselves, therefore, under God's mighty hand, that he may lift you up in due time. Cast all your anxiety on him because he cares for you.

When we humble ourselves under God's mighty hand, we are placing our trust in him, and not in ourselves. When we do this, we are able to cast our anxieties onto him, knowing that he will shoulder them for us. Peter, being a fisherman, uses a fishing term for "cast" that describes a fisherman casting his net away from the boat.

We cast, we throw our anxieties out and away from us, and onto Jesus, because we know Jesus cares about us with his great compassion.

Jesus and God the Father are interested and involved in the details:

This is perhaps Jesus' most comforting and endearing quality. Yes, I believe God Almighty is in control of the world, but is he interested, and will he get involved in the details of my life? Even in the details of a wedding? Will God Almighty, El Shaddai, actually help out with such a seemingly mundane problem as running out of wine?

Yes, and yes, and yes, absolutely he will.

HOW JESUS DOES THINGS

Jesus and God the Father do things like this:

> "Now to him who is able to do immeasurably more than all we ask or imagine."

When the wine runs out Jesus answers a felt need, with thousands of cups of choice wine. Is this perhaps a tad over the top? Perhaps. But if wine signifies joy, Jesus is showing us his joy is overflowing with spectacular wonder. And this is not unusual for Jesus. After all, when he takes a few fish and a little bread and feeds five thousand men, plus their families, he still has twelve baskets overflowing with extra bread.

And when he decided to get Peter's attention, he almost sunk two boats with hundreds of fish:

> When he had finished speaking, he said to Simon, "Put out into deep water, and let down the nets for a catch." When they had done so, they caught such a large number of fish that their nets began to break. So they signaled their partners in the other boat to come and help them, and they came and filled both boats so full that they began to sink.

Let's think for a moment about the choices Jesus had in this whole wedding affair.

1. He could have not gone to the wedding. He is, after all, the long-awaited Messiah. He has much to do to kick off his ministry. But Jesus is a relational God.

2. He could have said no to Mary.
   Please do not miss this: Jesus never says no, as in "No, I won't respond at all to your need."
   He may say, "No, I won't answer your specific request, because it would not be the best path for you."
   But he always responds, and always in the best way possible.

Now, as to how he could have responded, with respect to the 'Quantity & Quality' of wine:

3. He could have produced just barely enough wine, and ordinary wine at that. This would have saved the young bride and groom. And yet if it were just barely enough, they would still worry about running out again.

4. He could have produced more than enough wine, yet still just an average wine.

5. But three thousand cups of the *best wine*? Jesus is no bread and water God. He responds with, as Paul says in his letter to the Ephesians, "immeasurably more than all we ask or imagine."

And he will with you, too. To be sure, his blessings for me, i.e., my "immeasurably more than all we ask or imagine," will look different than yours, but it will be just right for me, and just right for you. Yes, his way and his timing may try our patience at times, but Jesus always responds with perfect timing, and always with the perfect, customized response to your need.

That is how Jesus does things.

I often think about how we view God. Is he God Almighty, all-powerful, but not very personal to you? Or is he a loving Heavenly Father, who is very personal, very compassionate, and very ... very generous? What I have concluded is it is not that we expect too much from God and are often disappointed, but that we expect too little, and so thus so often disappoint our Father with our meager expectations.

He is a lavish Father. But we are content with a little study of the scriptures, a little prayer, and a few blessings. Therefore, as Paul wrote in his letter to my fellow Ephesians,

> I keep asking that the God of our Lord Jesus Christ, the glorious Father, may give you the Spirit of wisdom and revelation, so that you may know him better.
>
> I pray that the eyes of your heart may be enlightened in order that you may know the hope to which he has called you, the riches of his glorious inheritance in his holy people, and his incomparably great power for us who believe.

So my question to you is this:

When you approach Jesus with your prayers, and your needs, which of the above 1 - 5 responses do you expect from Jesus? Do you think he will not even show up, or he will say no, or he will at best respond with just barely enough, and ordinary at that?

My friend, may you learn that Jesus always responds with immeasurably more than all we ask, or even imagine to ask, and may the eyes of your heart be enlightened so you may see his response as the wonderful gift it always is.

11

UP TO JERUSALEM

John 3

After this Jesus went down to Capernaum with his mother and brothers and his disciples. There we all stayed for a few days. During our time in Capernaum with Jesus, my big brother James and Andrew's big brother Peter began to spend more and more time with Jesus.

Peter begrudgingly so, but James' enthusiasm was growing. Jesus handled them both with the perfect combination of grace and salt. We will talk more about this "Grace and Salt" idea later, but let me explain briefly what I mean.

Everyone is different, individually, and yet everyone is the same, individually. Jesus knows what you need from him in all situations. He knows when you need salt – blunt truth – and knows when you need grace – a softer approach. With Peter, and his blunt, blusterous self, Jesus was more inclined to "punch him in the nose" with truth. With James, his approach was more grace-full.

Jesus knew Peter would respond better to straightforward challenges, and he knew James would respond better to a softer approach. So Andrew and I watched the master teacher draw them in, in much the same way we might bring a fish in. But bring them in he did, so that when it was time for the Passover feast, we all accompanied Jesus when he went up to Jerusalem.

By the way, we Jews say "Up to Jerusalem" because of her high elevation. No matter which route or approach one took, one was always walking up to the city. I wish you could have seen her glory as we approached the city, perched atop Mt Moriah, like a glorious eagle perched high atop her nest. She was indeed the City of God, bright shining on a hill.

Shortly after arriving we experienced firsthand Jesus' rampage through the temple courts, when he walked in and saw men selling cattle, sheep and doves, and others sitting at tables exchanging money. He was infuriated, and a wild look flashed in his eyes as he made a whip out of cords and proceeded to drive all of them from the temple courts, even the sheep and cattle.

He scattered the coins of the money changers and overturned their tables. To those who sold doves he said, "Get these out of here! Stop turning my Father's house into a market!"

Jesus was outraged, as angry as I ever saw him. It was as if it was a personal affront to him - a personal insult. He acted as if he owned the place. It was a chaotic scene as animals scurried around the temple platform, neighing and braying, birds flapping around and coins rolling down the floor.

It was a debacle of the highest order for the temple priests and leaders. He was making a mockery of them, and exposing them as the self-serving hypocrites they indeed were. Remember our honor-shame culture? This was a major shame for them, and I knew they would retaliate. They had to. And they would.

I could say more, but as I said at the outset of this story, I want to focus more on Jesus' encounters with various people. You can read about his temple outrage in the other three gospels. We had two key encounters coming up during our time in Jerusalem.

I would say that Jesus' encounter and conversation with Nicodemus in Jerusalem, and then with the Samaritan women on our way home from Jerusalem, might possibly represent God's entire scriptural story. This is a bold and broad-sweeping declaration, I know, but here is why I say this:

With Nicodemus, Jesus declares an essential maxim: "You must be born again."

With the Samaritan woman at the well, Jesus declares another essential maxim: "God is Spirit, and his worshipers must worship in the Spirit and in truth."

> "You must be born again."
> "Worshiping can only be with and through the Holy Spirit."

BORN AGAIN THROUGH THE HOLY SPIRIT

We will see that with Nicodemus, Jesus is adamant that we must all be born again. We must have a second birth. I remember once, after Jesus' ascension to the Father, Matthew and I were planning to teach about one of our experiences with Jesus. As we sat down to prepare and coordinate our comments, Matthew stopped me in mid-sentence and said, "Brother, before we even get into the details of this marvelous story, we must emphasize Jesus' insistence that, "You must be born again."

On that particular day of teaching, I was more focused on Jesus' encounter with the rich young ruler, and I wanted to jump right in and expand on his interaction with the young man. There were so many lessons to draw out of their exchange. But Matthew pulled me aside and said, "Brother, anything we teach means nothing to someone who is not born again."

Of course he was right. Without the Holy Spirit, teaching is just teaching. Without the Holy Spirit, no true worship can happen. Without the Holy Spirit, no one can receive true teaching from Jesus. Perhaps we would even call it self-help teaching and self-help worshiping, because without the Spirit, one can only try in one's Self-effort to ... *improve*. Improvement is not what we are after; a new heart and soul are.

And with the Samaritan woman at the well, Jesus emphasizes that where we worship, or what methods we use when we worship God, are secondary to our worshiping in Spirit and in truth. To Jesus, temples, holy mountains, and places and procedures for worship are entirely secondary to worshiping in and through the Holy Spirit.

Do you see the common thrust? The Holy Spirit. The Holy Spirit who indwells us, who compels us, who motivates us, and who empowers us. He teaches us all truth, but, only after we are born again.

PASSOVER

Now the Passover feast would draw tens of thousands, even hundreds of thousands of Jews from around Israel, as well as from all over the Diaspora - those Jews scattered around the Roman empire. (During our day more Jews lived outside Palestine than within.) Our family always made the trip together up to Jerusalem for Passover.

Even Peter would take off from his constant fishing to attend. This year Peter, Andrew, Nathaniel, Philip, James and I traveled with Jesus and his family. We were now his disciples, and where he went, we went. Oh, how I wish you could have seen Jerusalem in all its glory, and the magnificent temple Herod had enlarged and beautified beyond anything anywhere around.

The temple mount was huge – as large as Herod the Great's ego. But I must acknowledge what a tremendous builder and architectural visionary Herod was. He was a pig and a maniac, but he was indeed an incredible builder. The temple was simply glorious. And yet he had so many other incredible building projects that one could spend weeks studying them. For example, Masada, the man-made harbor at Caesarea, and his palace and fortress at Herodium. I encourage you to study them all. You will not be disappointed.

The city was buzzing with excitement, and as typical during this time, buzzing with talk of the expected Messiah. Each year we relished this time with our fellow Jews. During the seven-day festival our little band of *talmidim* (disciples) would spend most of each day in Jerusalem, visiting with friends, sharing a meal, and enjoying the crowds of fellow Jews. When we were at the temple there were always noted rabbis teaching around the temple mount, some in the Solomon's Porch area and some in the Royal Stoa.

On one occasion we walked by the noted Pharisee and teacher, Nicodemus, as he was teaching one morning in the Royal Stoa area. This is where the Sanhedrin met, so we would typically see a noted Pharisee teaching there. He was teaching from Ezekiel, which portended - by coincidence? - Jesus' stinging rebuke to him later that night.

During our trips to the temple over the years, Jesus would typically teach in the Solomon's Colonnade area. While Jesus was in Jerusalem at this Passover Festival, many people saw the signs he was performing and trusted in his name. They were fascinated by him.

But Jesus would not entrust himself to them, for he knew all men. He did not need man's testimony, and he could not be swayed by attention and adoration. He knew what was in men's hearts. He knew how fickle we can be. He knew everyone's heart. His lack of trust was not a discouraging thing to him. It did not cause him to be bitter. He simply knew better than to put his trust in any human being. Not even in us, his disciples; not even after our years together.

And of course he was absolutely right, because we all deserted him at his arrest, in his crucial time of need. But I have to tell you, Jesus was not suspicious of others, nor was he ever standoffish. Even though he knew the heart of all people, he did not close himself off to anyone. He was welcoming, and open, even when he knew their motive was untrustworthy. And why? Because he put his trust in God, first. He trusted absolutely in what God's grace could do for anyone.

So he never lost hope – his hope, his *confident expectation,* was in God's love, and the Holy Spirit's power to change and transform lives.

I want to pause here because this is a very important lesson. If we put our hope, our expectation, in anyone, we will be disappointed. If we put our absolute trust in someone, anyone, especially a wife or a husband, and expect them to always come through for us, we are setting ourselves up to be disappointed by them.

We are all only human. We will let people down. Even our loved ones. I have, you have, we all have. It is not a matter of being bad or good; it is a matter of being human.

Jesus did not put his trust in people, even when they were praising him, and worshiping him. But he was never bitter, and he never lost hope for anyone. He knew what God could do in anyone's life. He knew the transformation the Holy Spirit could bring about in anyone.

I have learned this lesson from Jesus, and over the years have learned to place all my trust in only Jesus. This does not mean I trust no one, and it certainly does not mean I am suspicious of everyone – what an awful way that would be to live. But it means I see others as the flawed human beings there are. And more importantly, I see myself the same way.

Why would I place my trust in any other human when I can hardly trust myself?

I believe this proper self-perception is a key aspect of the blessed commandment to, "Love your neighbor as yourself." If we dig into the rabbis' thinking on this, as well as our Jewish cultural idioms, we will see this commandment could be stated this way:

"Love your neighbor, for he is yourself."

In other words, we are to love our neighbors, even our enemies, because we are in fact no different, and certainly no better than them. They are us and we are them, at least in the eyes of a perfect God. If you think you are better than "Those other wretched people" you are deluded. Yes, of course your outward behavior may be better than someone else's, but God is not fooled by appearances. He sees the heart.

You can be good before the Lord, but you cannot be righteous. Not without Jesus, and not without being born again. Therefore in Christ Jesus we are all children of God through faith – through surrendering and placing our trust in him - for we who were baptized into Christ have been clothed with Christ. There is neither Jew nor Gentile, neither slave nor free, nor is there male and female, for we are all one in Christ Jesus.

For there is no difference between Jew and Gentile—the same Lord is Lord of all and richly blesses all who call on him, for, "Everyone who calls on the name of the Lord will be saved."

Nicodemus was about to find this out.

12

A NIGHT-TIME ENCOUNTER

John 3

Nicodemus was a Pharisee, a member of the Jewish ruling council. He came to Jesus one night seeking an audience with him. It was rumored Nicodemus was one of the top three richest men in Jerusalem. He preferred to be called by his Greek name, Nicodemus, which means he was proud of his Hellenistic (Greek) cultural status. He was a very important man, and his opinion in the Sanhedrin carried much weight. This made his coming to see our itinerant rabbi all the more curious.

I must tell you we were all surprised, shocked actually, at the arrival of such an important member of the Sanhedrin. The Sanhedrin was the ruling body of our nation. It was made up of Pharisees and Sadducees, many of whom were rich and important. The Sadducees were from the priestly line and were all rich and upper class, and therefore very prideful. They controlled the temple, and the profit and money generated by the selling of animals for sacrifice, and the exchanging of coins necessary for gifts to the temple. Jesus' earlier rampage through the Temple grounds would have threatened and insulted them the most.

The Sadducees also determined the selection of the Chief Priest each year, even though Rome was officially in charge of this, and controlled who the High Priest would be. The Chief Priest would preside over any "court cases" brought before the group. We will see this later in our story when Jesus is arrested that fateful night.

The Sadducees were corrupt and very much aligned with the Roman authorities. There was a constant tension between the Pharisees and the Sadducees. The Pharisees typically had jobs and professions, and they were more conservative and aligned with our Hebrew Scriptures.

The Sadducees recognized only the authority of the Pentateuch, the first five books of our Hebrew scriptures. They claimed this was because they rejected the Oral Law, which was so important to the Pharisees. (Can you see politics creeping in here?) The Oral Law was the Pharisees' attempt to put a hedge of protection around the written Law – our Pentateuch, our Torah. The Pharisees were well-meaning, but their Oral Laws were suffocating the life out of the Father's wonderful Torah teachings.

During Passover we spent our nights over on the Mount of Olives, in a spot near the Garden of Gethsemane. There was an olive grove there and a press for extracting the olive oil. Jesus loved this spot and would often sit and look over the Kidron Valley back to the city.

I vividly remember sitting next to Jesus one evening as he looked over to Jerusalem and watching him as he seemed lost in thought. His eyes ranged back and forth across the city and I remember hearing a slight grunt from him as they did. He was shaking his head, just barely perceptible, but as he did he groaned. At the time I did not know what was on his mind, but later he would declare his love and his sorrow for his Father's beloved city:

> "Jerusalem, Jerusalem, you who kill the prophets and stone those sent to you, how often I have longed to gather your children together, as a hen gathers her chicks under her wings, and you were not willing. Look, your house is left to you desolate. I tell you, you will not see me again until you say, 'Blessed is he who comes in the name of the Lord.'"

The nights were cool and refreshing on the Mount of Olives, and were a welcome change after a day on the warmer, crowded streets of the city. That night when Nicodemus came to visit there were campfires all around us, spotted all over the hillside on the Mount of Olives, with pilgrims everywhere.

We were sitting around our campfire listening to Peter tell a fishing story, exaggerating no doubt, as he was often wont to do. Jesus was laughing along with all of us as Andrew rolled his eyes and said, "Big brother, you have told that story dozens of times, and it seems each time the fish get bigger, as well as the muscles in your strong arms as you fight to bring it in!"

Peter made a funny scowl and balled his fists and Andrew raised his hands in mock surrender. It was a typical night of good friends enjoying each other's company. I heard someone approaching our little band of brothers and looked up to see young John Mark approaching with a distinguished-looking man.

Nicodemus cleared his throat to get our attention and the rest looked up. He had been led to us by this young boy, John Mark, who would follow us around the temple each day. Young John Mark would one day be a valuable member of our group. His family was part of the upper class of Jerusalem and later we would meet at his mother's home.

Jesus regarded this important Pharisee for a moment, smiled slightly, then motioned for us to make room for our new arrival. We shifted around and Nicodemus sat down across the fire from Jesus. The stars were bright and the moon was full. The conversations from those sitting around their fires seemed to fade away as I waited for this important man to speak.

Nicodemus shifted in his seat, looked at each of us, and then directed his attention to Jesus. He cleared his throat, and then said, "Rabbi, we can see that you are a teacher who has come from God. For no one could perform the signs you are doing if God were not with him."

I was watching Jesus closely, trying to discern his thought process and his reaction to this surprising arrival. But Jesus did not seem surprised at all. He looked calmly at this prestigious man, smiled, and replied,

> "Very truly I tell you, no one can see the kingdom of God unless they are born again."

BORN AGAIN?

My first thought, and probably Nicodemus' as well, was, "What does that have to do with Nicodemus' opening comment?" Nicodemus started by complimenting Jesus, yet Jesus practically cuts him off with a seemingly unrelated response. But I now realize Jesus was responding directly to Nicodemus' statement, "We can see you are a teacher who has come from God." Jesus was saying, "You cannot *see* anything about me, Nicodemus, and you cannot *see* anything about kingdom of God until you are born again."

Nicodemus looked confused and did not say anything for a moment. The silence was uncomfortable. But then he lifted his arms in a sign of frustration and asked, "How can someone be born when they are old? I am an old man. Surely I cannot enter a second time into my mother's womb to be born again?"

Nicodemus' confusion brings to mind Paul's statement to the Corinthians in his first letter:

> The person without the Spirit does not accept the things that come from the Spirit of God but considers them foolishness, and cannot understand them because they are discerned only through the Spirit.

This talk about being born again sounded like foolishness to Nicodemus. He could not understand what Jesus was saying, because no one knows the thoughts of God except the Spirit of God. What we have received from Jesus is not the spirit of the world, which is all Nicodemus had, but the Spirit who is from God, so that we may understand what God has freely given us, not in words taught us by human wisdom but in words taught by the Spirit.

Nicodemus was not being disrespectful; he was honestly perplexed. He began to speak but then sat back in silence. He just could not accept this idea of a grown man being born a second time. And how could he? Neither could I. We did not yet have the Holy Spirit. We had not yet been born again.

I could see Jesus was drawing Nicodemus in, slowly but surely. He then said, "Very truly I tell you, no one can enter the kingdom of God unless they are born of water and the Spirit. Flesh gives birth to flesh, but the Spirit gives birth to spirit." Now Nicodemus was visibly frustrated. He stared into the fire, and then back up at Jesus. He was trying to sort out this new teaching. He knew Jesus was a man sent from God, but he was nowhere close to understanding that Jesus was in fact, God. Not sent from - is. I felt sympathy for this learned man, dressed in his temple regalia. He was not accustomed to being the student.

A soft breeze wafted across our fire, causing it to flicker. Was it the Holy Spirit? The stars seemed to flicker as well, as Jesus leaned toward Nicodemus, lifted his arms slightly, palms up and said, with a somewhat sardonic tone, "You should not be surprised at my saying, 'You must be born again.'" He looked around, taking in the breeze, and said, "The wind blows wherever it pleases. You hear its sound, but you cannot tell where it comes from or where it is going. So it is with everyone born of the Spirit."

"How can this be?" Nicodemus asked.

As I said, at the time I was as confused as anyone, but now looking back I can see exactly what Jesus was saying about the Spirit and the wind. He was using wordplay. Our Hebrew word for wind is the same as for spirit. Even the Greek word for spirit, "pneuma," can mean spirit, wind or breath. And yes, the Holy Spirit is not visible, and his ways are not quantitative and easily definable – much like the wind.

But just as we see the wind moving, we see his moving. When one has been indwelled with the Spirit, when the Spirit is living inside you, you know it. Like the wind, you may not can see it physically, but you see and feel it moving, and you see and feel the effect of it. The Spirit is as real as the wind, and his movements are as obvious as the wind – for those with eyes to see and hearts to feel him.

Jesus continued as he leaned toward Nicodemus. "You are Israel's teacher, and do you not understand these things?" His tone wasn't condemning, but it was challenging.

At this point, like Nicodemus, we were all mystified. He opened his mouth then shut it. Peter shifted nervously, and my brother James looked out across the valley towards the city. Nathanael and Philip exchanged quizzical looks, but I noticed young Andrew was transfixed on Nicodemus. Andrew told me later he had never before sat in the company of such a wealthy and important man, and to see him so befuddled was a wonder to him.

But why, you might ask, did Jesus say Nicodemus should have "understood these things?" To be fair there is no mention of "being born again" in our Hebrew scriptures. Jesus was bringing what I thought was a completely new teaching. But he was not. Do not miss that: He was not bringing a new teaching. Nicodemus should have known. Throughout our scriptures the idea of a new beginning for the Father's children, with the Spirit being poured out, is evident.

From the time Adam and Eve "died" in the Genesis story, all mankind has been stillborn spiritually. Adam and Eve did not physically die immediately after they ate the forbidden fruit, but they immediately died spiritually – now separated from their Creator. They were separated from God. Since then, everyone is born spiritually separated from God. You recall I stated this plainly in my opening prologue:

> Yet to all who did receive him, to those who believed in his name, he gave the right to become children of God— children born not of natural descent, nor of human decision or a husband's will, but born of God.

We all must *become* children of God – through a second birth.

Just think about Ezekiel's prophecies that Nicodemus would have memorized, and "just so happened" to be teaching about that very morning:

> I will give you a new heart and put a new spirit in you; I will remove from you your heart of stone and give you a heart of flesh. And I will put my Spirit in you and move you to follow my decrees and be careful to keep my laws.

Ezekiel then has a vision of the valley of dry ... dead ... bones, which immediately follows this prophecy, as if to illustrate what God is saying. God says he will bring them back to life. Back to life, because they are dead. In essence, they will be born again, with the Holy Spirit:

> He asked me, "Son of man, can these bones live?" Then he said to me: "Son of man, these bones are the people of Israel. They say, 'Our bones are dried up and our hope is gone; we are cut off.'

> "Therefore prophesy and say to them: 'This is what the Sovereign LORD says: My people, I am going to open your graves and bring you up from them; I will bring you back to the land of Israel. Then you, my people, will know that I am the LORD, when I open your graves and bring you up from them.
>
> "I will put my Spirit in you and you will live, and I will settle you in your own land. Then you will know that I the LORD have spoken, and I have done it, declares the LORD.'"

Our prophet Joel speaks to this:

> "And afterward, I will pour out my Spirit on all people.
> Your sons and daughters will prophesy, your old men will dream dreams,
> your young men will see visions.
> Even on my servants, both men and women, I will pour out my Spirit in those days."

Nicodemus should have been able to put all this together, to understand that God was promising a new life, a second life, a reborn life, with the Holy Spirit now inside the Believer - permanently. Later, in a confrontation with other Pharisees, Jesus chided them by saying,

> "You study the Scriptures diligently because you think that in them you have eternal life. These are the very Scriptures that testify about me, yet you refuse to come to me to have life."

I know Nicodemus had diligently studied the scriptures all his life. He was sincere, just sincerely wrong. Like so many, he had missed God's message of restoration, rebirth, and renewal.

Nicodemus was rebuked by Jesus not because there was a particular passage in our Hebrew scriptures that escaped his notice, but because Nicodemus should have known from the overarching message of our Hebrew scriptures that people must be spiritually born again to enter the Kingdom of God.

He should have known that we are all born spiritually dead, and the only hope for a dead man is a resurrection. The only hope for the spiritually dead is to be born again with the Spirit who is alive, the Spirit from above.

13

NICODEMUS – "YOU MUST BE ..."

John 3

By this point Nicodemus seemed a bit disoriented, yet he was listening intently for what might come next. Jesus continued, looking directly into Nicodemus' eyes,

> "Very truly I tell you, we speak of what we know, and we testify to what we have seen, but still you people do not accept our testimony. Just as Moses lifted up the snake in the wilderness, so the Son of Man must be lifted up, that everyone who believes may have eternal life in him."

Nicodemus leaned in and almost interrupted Jesus. His eyes brightened a bit, and he said, "You are referring to the story in Numbers, about Moses saving the Israelites in the desert after they spoke against God." Then Nicodemus leaned back and closed his eyes and began to recite the scriptures, word for word:

> They traveled from Mount Hor along the route to the Red Sea, to go around Edom. But the people grew

> impatient on the way; they spoke against God and against Moses, and said, "Why have you brought us up out of Egypt to die in the wilderness? There is no bread! There is no water! And we detest this miserable food!"
>
> Then the LORD sent venomous snakes among them; they bit the people and many Israelites died. The people came to Moses and said, "We sinned when we spoke against the LORD and against you. Pray that the LORD will take the snakes away from us." So Moses prayed for the people.
>
> The LORD said to Moses, "Make a snake and put it up on a pole; anyone who is bitten can look at it and live." So Moses made a bronze snake and put it up on a pole. Then when anyone was bitten by a snake and looked at the bronze snake, they lived.

Jesus listened patiently. When Nicodemus finished Jesus paused, smiled, and said,

> "For God so loved the world that he gave his one and only Son, that whoever believes in him shall not perish but have eternal life. For God did not send his Son into the world to condemn the world, but to save the world through him. Whoever believes in him is not condemned, but whoever does not believe stands condemned already because they have not believed in the name of God's one and only Son."

Nicodemus considered this for a moment, then said, "So rabbi, I take it you are saying you are this "one and only Son"? And you are calling yourself 'Son of Man,' the figure we read about in Daniel? You are comparing yourself with Moses lifting up the bronze snake for the Israelites to look at to be saved?

Teacher, you obviously realize the implications of such statements."

He looked around our little group, paused, and then said, "You are in effect calling yourself God's Son. My fellow Sanhedrin members would consider that blasphemy in the highest order. Are you prepared for the maelstrom you are inviting upon yourself?"

Jesus remained silent, so Nicodemus continued, "And I must say, I just do not understand what you mean by this talk of God giving his Son for the world? But I came here to hear from you, to understand who you are, so I will hold these questions for now."

THE NEW BIRTH

I would like to pause here in the middle of their conversation and take a few minutes to expand on this most important interchange between the Master and the master Pharisee. You will recall I said earlier that Jesus' encounter and conversation with Nicodemus, and then his next encounter with the Samaritan women at the well, might possibly represent God's entire scriptural story. Therefore, we will spend more time examining the teaching lessons to be found in these two encounters than we will, perhaps in all the other encounters combined.

Since Jesus' death, we the Twelve began to grasp more and more the implications of Jesus saying, "You must be born again." The idea of this new birth took hold and was repeated by Peter, Paul and James (Jesus' little brother), in their letters to fellow believers.

Peter said in his first letter,

> "Praise be to the God and Father of our Lord Jesus Christ! In his great mercy he has given us *new birth* into a living hope through the resurrection of Jesus Christ from the dead." For you have been *born again,*

> not of perishable seed, but of imperishable, through the living and enduring word of God."

Paul wrote in his second letter to the Corinthians,

> Therefore, if anyone is in Christ, he is a *new creation*. The old has gone, the new is here!

And James put it like this,

> He chose to give us *birth* through the word of truth, that we might be a kind of firstfruits of all he created.

I know I am saying, "Peter said …," and, "Paul wrote …," and, "James said …," but the reality is it was the Holy Spirit speaking through them. You must understand that no prophecy of Scripture came about by the prophet's own interpretation of things. For prophecy never had its origin in the human will, but prophets, though human, spoke from God as they were carried along by the Holy Spirit.

Now please notice Jesus said, "You must be born again." He did not say, "It would be helpful in your life as a Christian to be born again." He did not say, "For anyone who wants to be an advanced follower of Jesus you must be born again." He did not say, "It is a good idea to be born again."

No, he said, "You must," because he meant *you must*. You must be born again to even see the Kingdom of God, much less enter it. Did you notice that? Jesus first said, "No one can see the kingdom of God unless he is born again." He then said, "No one can enter the kingdom of God unless he is born again."

To me it is common sense that one cannot enter someplace one cannot see. So how do we have our eyes opened so we can see the kingdom of God? We must be born again … with the Holy Spirit. We do not see the kingdom of God with our physical eyes; we see with the eyes of our heart. Paul stated this clearly in his letter to the church in Ephesus, the very same Family of Followers I now guide:

> I pray that the eyes of your heart may be enlightened in order that you may know the hope to which he has called you, the riches of his glorious inheritance in his holy people, and his incomparably great power for us who believe.

The Holy Spirit opens the eyes of our hearts when we are born again. We then do not just *see* the kingdom; we are *in* the kingdom. We become the kingdom!

In the ensuing years there have been those who have tried to get around Jesus' declarative imperative by trying to water it down. I have heard people try to use the multiple meanings of our Hebrew word, "ruach," which as I said can mean spirit, wind, or even breath. They try to cast doubt on Jesus' adamant statement.

And because Jesus' statement, "You must be born again," could also be understood to mean, "You must be born from above," these same people attempt to evade the simple truth by saying, "Well, Jesus could have meant born from above, which might mean a spiritual awakening or something like that."

I see right through them. They are just trying to avoid the blunt truth of Jesus' declarative imperative, because ... simply put, they are not born again.

I have observed that people do not like the term "Born again" for a variety of reasons – all having to do with pride. The Jews certainly do not like this term. It offends their pride to suggest they are like everyone else, gentiles and pagans alike, who surely are not born "children of God."

The intellectuals scoff at this term, as well. Over the years many very smart men have told me, "I prefer the intellectual approach. I like to study the scriptures and the history of it all, and to discuss the various interpretations." To one such man I simply replied, "There are going to be a lot of intellectuals in hell, my friend."

Remember, Jesus said,

> "You study the Scriptures diligently because you think that in them you have eternal life. These are the very Scriptures that testify about me, yet you refuse to come to me to have life."

I would say that about sums it up, wouldn't you?

14

HOW GOOD IS GOOD ENOUGH?

John 3

And the religious – the *really good* people – also do not like the term "born again." They prefer instead to make a list of their synagogue and temple and community accomplishments and activities. They would never say this out loud, but they are not going to lower themselves to accept the free gift of salvation. No, they will earn it by being good enough. Not perfect, mind you, but good enough to make it to Heaven. Especially compared to everyone else.

But the simple truth is this: How good is good enough?

The rich young ruler knew he was good, very good, actually, but in his heart he was struggling with how good is good enough? So he went to see Jesus with the hope Jesus would either define *good enough,* or assuage his concerns by telling him he was indeed good enough.

I once listened to a couple of well-dressed, smart and successful, Hellenistic Jewish men arguing with my fellow disciples. Hellenistic just means they acted more Greek than Hebrew. These men wanted to be associated with King Herod more than with the Jews. With their condescending pride barely masked, they sneered, "Being born again is for you Galilean country types, or for those who have failed in life. You experienced some collapse in your life and so you turn to Jesus with all this emotion, pleading, 'Save me, Jesus!' You need a crutch. That's all Jesus is to you: a crutch."

"Yes," his companion continued, "I am not saying I'm perfect, but I'm not all that bad, either. I have never had such a flame-out. I am still married; I am still providing for my family with my hard work. I helped build the new meeting place, and I was in charge of raising money and supplies for our families who were suffering through that awful famine a few years back. The one for which Saul was raising money.

SPIRITUALLY BANKRUPT

Now if I could get them to listen, really listen with ears to hear, I would remind them of Jesus' very first words we find in Matthew's account of Jesus' "Sermon on the Mount:"

> "Blessed are the poor in spirit, for theirs is the kingdom of heaven."

Jesus is saying, "Blessed are you when you see your spiritual poverty – when you see that you are spiritually bankrupt without me. Then and only then will you see your need for a Savior. Your *desperate* need for a savior. Then and only then will you see yourself for who you are: a wretched, prideful, rebellious sinner."

Few are willing to see themselves as rebels. As a matter of fact, it takes the Holy Spirit to convict them, to bruise their pride, to … expose them.

Those who dislike the term born again do not think they are spiritually bankrupt at all, nor would they think of themselves as rebels, or even sinners, and certainly not *wretched* sinners. No, they think they just need a little polishing up.

They deceive themselves with the idea that Jesus would actually be doing pretty darn good for them to "accept him," to make a decision for him, because they think they bring much to the table.

Ha! I used to think that way. I used to think in terms of my being partners with Jesus. And yes, with the Holy Spirit indwelling me, I am indeed a partner with Jesus. But way back then I thought of being equal partners with Jesus. I thought Jesus would benefit from my advice and leadership.

These intellectuals and religious do-gooder men and women think in terms of "accepting Jesus," as in agreeing to join Jesus' board of advisors. Surely you can see just how ridiculous this is.

One more observation about being born again: You will know when it happens. Maybe there will be blinding lights or a choir of angels singing, or maybe not. (Probably not) Perhaps you will be sitting alone, and the light simply gets brighter in your heart. But when this happens, however it happens, you will know it, and you will remember it.

You will remember a specific day. Or perhaps a specific season, but the season will not be years, or even months. It will be a very specific season, and it will always remain vivid in your mind. It is not a decade, or "sometime in my 40's," and it is definitely not, "I've been a Christian all my life."

No one has been a Christian all their life. Remember, you were not born a Christian. You must be reborn a Christian. If you do not know a day or time or a season when you were born again, you likely are not.

Perhaps this all this sounds extreme to you, or even harsh. I understand that. I will apologize for my bluntness, but not for the message. Jesus said it like this on our last night together:

> In just a little while the world will no longer see me, but you are going to see me because I am alive and you're about to come alive. At that moment you will

> know absolutely that I'm in my Father, and you're in me, and I'm in you.

Yes, at that moment of your salvation, you will know absolutely that you have been born again.

My dear child, please do not try to water down Jesus' words, and please do not try to evade the issue. It is too critical. Anyone who has been born again knows exactly what Jesus is saying. Their eyes have been opened because the Holy Spirit opens the eyes of their hearts, and they can finally see.

A TERRIBLE TRANSLATION: BELIEVE

Bear with me, because I must also comment on Jesus' statement to Nicodemus,

> "For God so loved the world that he gave his one and only Son, that whoever believes in him shall not perish but have eternal life. Whoever believes in him is not condemned, but whoever does not believe stands condemned already because they have not believed in the name of God's one and only Son."

Jesus spoke Aramaic and Hebrew, but I write to you in Greek. A very unfortunate error has occurred over the years. It is such a grievous error I fear it will send large numbers of men and women to Hell – a very real place.

The translation error is the word "believe." Our Hebrew word for believe is "emunah." The Greek word is "pistueo." Both these words carry a deep meaning of trust, dependence, and surrender. "Believing information" is not what Jesus means. Believing a set of facts about Jesus is not at all what Jesus means.

Let me tell you what Jesus is actually saying:

> "Whoever surrenders their heart and their will to the Son shall not perish but have eternal life. Whoever places their trust in, and their entire dependence upon the Son is not condemned .... Whoever transfers their trust from their own ability to be good enough to make it into Heaven, to the Son and his righteousness, shall have eternal life."

To be born again is a matter of surrender. We surrender our right to ourselves. We surrender any claim we think we have to any good works, and we fall on our knees and ask Jesus to transfer his purity, his righteousness and his salvation to us. We place our entire and utter dependence on Jesus to save us.

DESPERATE AND SURRENDER.

We will only do this when we are desperate. *Desperate and surrender*. This is the key. Until you are desperate, you will see no need for surrender. Instead, you may think this: "I am not that bad. Oh sure, I am not perfect. I could use a little polishing up. But surrender? I do not even like that word. It sounds like defeat. No, surrender is for those who have really crashed in life. They are the desperate ones. I am not desperate."

But my friend, you are. You are desperate. You just cannot see it. Your sins may not be as evident for all to see, but you are a sinner, separated from God, and you need to be saved. You desperately need to be saved.

It is never about 'believe.' As Jesus' brother James says, "You believe that there is one God. Good! Even the demons believe that—and shudder."

15

NICODEMUS: PERFECT LOVE

John 3

I have been blunt with you, but only as blunt as Jesus. So let me return to the overarching message of Jesus, and of God the Father: Love.

> "For God so loved the world, he sent and he gave his only Son to die for you and for me."

As you know I am called by many, "The Disciple Whom Jesus Loved." And as you know this is what I call myself. Not because I feel more loved by Jesus than my fellow disciples, but because his love for me has been my North star all these years. His love for me first knocked me out of my fishing boat; his love for me then carried me during our years together; and now his love for me compels me, and even propels me, to carry on his name and his mission for all these years.

I am an old man now, and his love has only deepened with time. You can surely understand why I will surely spend a little time on this statement Jesus made to Nicodemus.

I want you to know the breathtaking scope of God the Father's love for you. I want you to feel his amazing love for you. Yes, he so loved *the world* he sent Jesus to die for our sins. But you, my friend, are *his world*. He loves *you*. You, reading this now. You, with all your faults and frailties. You, with all your selfishness.

He so loves you that he sent his only son, the son he so dearly loves, for you.

Is there anything more important for you to grasp than this? Is there any other fact that overrides this simple, foundational truth? You could memorize the entire Hebrew scriptures. You could give all your money away. You could, like our nighttime visitor, become, "The teacher of Israel." But without grasping this truth, this fact, and then appropriating it into the flow of your life, all that would have no meaning.

Paul captures this perfectly in his greeting at the beginning of his first letter to the Family in Thessalonica:

> We remember before our God and Father your work produced by faith, your labor prompted by love, and your endurance inspired by hope in our Lord Jesus Christ.

Your work – produced by trust.

Your labor – prompted by love.

Work is not only our normal day-to-day living and breathing, but also our professions, as well as sharing the good news of the Kingdom. I take great joy in this, and yes, it is indeed a natural product of my trust in Jesus.

But there are times when this day-to-day '*work*' becomes a laborious effort. Perhaps I am interacting with a particularly unpleasant person. There are many, I am sure you know, even in our Family of Followers. Perhaps I am confronted with hostility. These are the times when Jesus' love for me kicks in, and I am prompted by the Holy Spirit to share and show this same love to others – those unpleasant folks, as well as my so-called enemies.

His love prompts me to think not about what a labor it is to love others, but instead to think about how unpleasant I have been to others, even at times to my Savior. And when I grow weary, which I do at times, my endurance is inspired by hope - my hope, my confident expectation - in our Lord Jesus Christ.

As I said, hope means *confident expectation*. Not wishful or hopeful thinking. With his perfect love saturating my very existence, my confident expectation of his perfect love inspires me and energizes me.

In my first letter from here in Ephesus to our Family of Followers I said this:

> We love because he first loved us.
>
> This is love: not that we loved God, but that he loved us and sent his Son as an atoning sacrifice for our sins. Dear friends, since God so loved us, we also ought to love one another. No one has ever seen God; but if we love one another, God lives in us and his love is made complete in us.

God's love for me, and Jesus' life-changing love for me, propels me to love you. Without the flood of his love washing over me and through me, I can only love those who love me, and those who make me feel good about myself. That, my friend, is not Jesus' love. I continued in my letter:

> And so we know and rely on the love God has for us. God is love. Whoever lives in love lives in God, and God in them. This is how love is made complete among us so that we will have confidence on the day of judgment: In this world we are like Jesus.

In this world, we can become heirs to the first-born Son, becoming family members – bearing the family resemblance. This is Jesus' love reaching completion. Of course, this is a process, and I am still growing in his love, and therefore I am still growing in my love for others. But without God the Father first loving me, and Jesus showing me this love in real life, I would likely be growing only in self-love.

In my first letter the Holy Spirit prompted me to write:

> There is no fear in love. But perfect love drives out fear, because fear has to do with punishment. The one who fears is not made perfect in love.

Do you see it, the gem hidden here? "Perfect love drives out fear." Drives it out and drives it away! Jesus tells us God the Father loves us perfectly. Perfectly! Jesus then lived out this perfect love. This is why I call myself the disciple whom Jesus loved. If you have ever been in the presence of perfect love, and you are when you become a Kingdom Family member, you lose all fear. There is simply no room in your heart for fear. It has been driven out by love. His love. His perfect love. Fear loses all power over me. Instead of reacting in fear I now respond in faith because of his perfect love.

REACT IN FEAR OR RESPOND IN FAITH?

I remember so well Jesus telling us on his last night with us before his crucifixion,

> "I have told you these things, so that in me you may have peace. In this world you will have trouble. But take heart! I have overcome the world."

Yes, in this life we will have trouble. I have had plenty. I have lived through my brother James' murder. Stephen was stoned to death. I have lived through the execution of my dear brothers in Christ, Simon Peter and Paul. Mary has died. I have been tortured, ostracized and even exiled from my beloved homeland.

But with each of these very scary life situations, I have learned more and more to focus on the facts of my faith:

Fact 1: Jesus has overcome the world

Fact 2: He loves me perfectly

Fact 3: He is always with me, even to the very end of the age

Fact 4: There is nothing, not one thing, that will ever happen to me that Jesus is not aware of and in control of

Fact 5: From Saul's letter to the Roman Christians, "And we know that in all things God works for the good of those who love him ..."

So why would I worry? Why would I react in fear, instead of responding in faith, in trust? I will, only when I let my feelings take over. Feelings promote fear; fear promotes reacting, which is almost always over-reacting. Over-reacting promotes mistakes.

I can choose to trust in these facts, and the character of my Savior, or I can choose to allow fear to overwhelm me.

Isn't that our choice in any difficult situation: to choose to trust, or choose to not trust? It is a choice after all. And remember, whenever you see the word faith, I want you to think of trust. That is what Jesus means by faith: trust.

I used to *react* to everything, good or bad. My feelings were my master, therefore reacting was all I knew. As I have grown in my trust, and the Spirit has filled me with the rock-solid awareness that I live in a God-saturated world, my feelings are no longer in control, and my trust is now leading the way.

FACTS – FAITH – FEELINGS

Faith, feelings and facts: how should a Follower of Jesus prioritize these?

Most would automatically place faith first, then muddle around with their answer between feelings and facts. Many of you would place facts last because you think faith trumps facts. Blind faith! I used to think this way. And with such an emphasis on faith among Jesus' followers, many think facts are anathema to faith.

No doubt many outsiders think we are even afraid of the facts. They are wrong. We are not only unafraid of the facts, but my order of priority is facts first, then faith, then feelings a distant third. Feelings are okay as servants, but they are terrible masters.

Remember Jesus taught us,

> "Are not two sparrows sold for a penny? Yet not one of them will fall to the ground outside your Father's care …"

Not one thing happens apart from or outside the will of my Father. That is a fact. I know I can trust that. If I find myself in a dangerous situation, my Father did not miss it. He does not turn around and say, "Oh no, I didn't see that coming. John has really gotten himself in a mess. I'm not sure what to do now."

I know that sounds laughable to you, but think about it - isn't this what worrying is all about? When you think this way, you are reacting in fear, because you are letting your feelings lead the way. Feelings are disastrous masters. They can certainly be positive as servants, but disastrous as masters.

Now this is going to sting a bit, and I am certainly not judging you. I can only say this because I have seen it in myself. When we fear, we might as well say to Jesus, "I have decided not to trust you, and instead to trust Satan. Because I find you to be untrustworthy, Jesus, and I find Satan to be much more trustworthy."

I know it stings, but do not sluff it off.

This is exactly what happened in the Garden of Eden. God actually walked with Adam and Eve. Can you imagine that? I can, because he walked with me, too, in the form of Jesus. Adam and Eve walked with God the Father, I walked with God the Son. Now we all can walk with God the Spirit.

God promised Adam and Eve anything and everything. But Satan came along and said, "You cannot really trust God. You cannot really trust he has your best interests in mind. God is trying to prohibit you from living your life to the full."

Adam and Eve trusted Satan over God. And that is precisely what you are doing when you succumb to fear. Your feelings take over and you totally ignore the facts: the promises of both Jesus and God the Father. I understand this process only too well. Before I learned to live with the power of the Spirit, fear was a stronghold for me as well.

TAKE CAPTIVE THOUGHTS

Brother Paul likes to say,

> For though we live in the world, we do not wage war as the world does. The weapons we fight with are not the weapons of the world. On the contrary, they have divine power to demolish strongholds. So we take captive every thought to make it obedient to Christ.

Peter and I were arrested more than once by the Sanhedrin following Jesus' death. The first arrest was my first arrest, and it had the potential to be very scary. As we sat in that cell, looking at the weapons of the world - the guards with their swords and daggers, and the iron chains around our hands - I heard the Holy Spirit saying, "Fear not, John. I am here with you; I am here *in* you. And I can demolish this prison anytime I choose. But allow me to first demolish your prison of fear. Allow me to first demolish your prison of feelings."

This is why I place the facts first, then my faith. I am a mere man, just like you. I can and I do feel fear. But my guess is I am not like you, in the sense I now choose – and it is my choice and your choice – to focus on the facts instead of my feelings. As I do this my faith, my trust, strengthens and my fear and anxiety diminish.

I can do this only by "taking captive every thought to make it obedient to Christ." As I sat in that cell with Simon, all those years ago, my feelings wanted to take over. My feelings were trying to conduct a mutiny over my faith. The thoughts in my head were reminding me of Jesus' gruesome death at the hands of these same men. Satan was telling me I am a nobody, and these powerful men hold my fate in their hands.

Can you see this is what Satan wanted me to believe? But who will I … choose … to believe?

When these thoughts of fear start to overwhelm me, and my feelings try to take over I have learned to grab those thoughts, wrestle them down, take them captive, and cast them aside. Yes, I was scared in that cell. To be transparent with you I felt a surge of panic wanting to take over.

But instead of reacting in fear, I chose to calmly respond in faith. So I looked at Simon and smiled, and raised my eyes toward Heaven and said, "Thank you now, Lord, before we see what you are going to do here, because we know we will be thanking you later."

This is an exercise that has revolutionized my faith journey. When my feelings try to take over, and my faith starts to wobble, I stop and say out loud, "Thank you now, Father. Before I see how you work this out. Because I know I will be thanking you later. Because you always bring good out of every situation."

Always. And with this statement of faith my trust strengthens and my fear weakens. Because I know he loves me perfectly. And perfect love drives out all fear. Try it!

16

NICODEMUS: LIGHT & DARKNESS

John 3

The night was getting cooler, so we gathered up some more branches and threw them on our fire. The flames sparked a bit as the branches lit up. The stars were in full regalia, and the moon cast a beautiful glow across Jerusalem. Fires were dotting the landscape of the hillside. That gentle breeze was still moving around us. I could have easily fallen asleep, were it not for this fascinating conversation between Nicodemus and Jesus.

Nicodemus seemed to be settling into Jesus' words, "For God so loved the world." He understood God's perfect love. I am certain Nicodemus taught many times about God's love and compassion. Throughout our Hebrew scriptures God expresses who he is, how he does things, and what he cares about. Just one of so many such passages is found in our book of Exodus:

> The Lord, the Lord, the compassionate and gracious God, slow to anger, abounding in love and faithfulness, maintaining love to thousands, and forgiving wickedness, rebellion and sin.

Nicodemus nodded his head in approval and motioned for Jesus to continue. Jesus' eyes narrowed and he leaned in, raising his arms again, his voice rising as he said,

> "This is the verdict: Light has come into the world, but people loved darkness instead of light because their deeds were evil. Everyone who does evil hates the light and will not come into the light for fear that their deeds will be exposed. But whoever lives by the truth comes into the light, so that it may be seen plainly that what they have done has been done in the sight of God."

Nicodemus smiled and said, "I do understand about light and darkness, rabbi, and you are exactly right about evil loving darkness and truth loving light." He then stood up and exclaimed with a smile, "At last I understand something you are saying! Perhaps this is a good time for me to take my leave."

Jesus stood and stepped around the fire, putting his hand on Nicodemus' shoulder. He looked him in the eye and said, "This is not farewell, my new friend. We will see each other again, and you will have all your questions answered. But as for tonight, here is what I want you to know:

"The Son of God loves you.

"He is on your side.

"He is coming after you.

"He is relentless."

Nicodemus looked into Jesus' eyes for an extended moment. They seemed to communicate something with each other. Time stood still. I could sense deep calling unto deep. He then nodded his head, turned, and walked away into the darkness.

As I watched Nicodemus fade into the darkness, Jesus' words about light and dark echoed in my mind. I wondered, would he stay in the darkness, or enter into Jesus' Light?

When Nicodemus left, we gathered in close around the fire and started quizzing Jesus about his encounter with this important man. Simon Peter asked, "What does it mean, Master, that such a man comes to see you – and at night? Do you think he is acting as a spy? Is he trying to find something with which to accuse you before the Sanhedrin?"

We all nodded and leaned in to hear Jesus' reply. He sat quietly for a moment. He then smiled and said, "This man is no different than you, my friends. He knows there is more to his religion than what he has experienced up to now. He knows there has to be more, and he senses I have that 'more' he is looking for. What he does not yet know is that not only do I have the more he is looking for, *I am* that more!"

He then sat back and said, "Nicodemus will become a follower, and he will assist us." We all guffawed at that thought, but Jesus maintained a serious expression. "I tell you the truth, Nicodemus will both defend me before the Sanhedrin, and he will one day risk his life for me."

Nicodemus did indeed become a follower of Jesus, albeit mostly a quiet one. But he did defend Jesus before the Sanhedrin when things were heating up at the Feast of Tabernacles. The Chief Priest had sent his guards to arrest Jesus, but they came back flummoxed by his mere presence. As the august body of learned men hurled insults around the room about Jesus, Nicodemus, in a remarkable display of courage, asked, "Does our law condemn a man without first hearing him to find out what he has been doing?"

The Sanhedrin's response? "Are you from Galilee, too? Look into it, and you will find that a prophet does not come out of Galilee."

And after Jesus' crucifixion Nicodemus joined Joseph, his fellow Sanhedrin member from Arimathea, in taking Jesus' body off the cross and providing a decent burial. By doing this he was publicly aligning himself with Jesus, exposing himself to ridicule, ostracization, and possible ex-communication.

Nicodemus later told me why he first came to see Jesus that night and what happened in his life afterward. He said, "I had heard that Jesus and John the Immerser were related, and I was eager to know if Jesus' approach was the same as John's approach of immersing adult Jews. I was at first confused as to why John would be immersing adult Jews and I was confused by his insistence on repentance. Only proselytes and other converts were typically immersed in water in our ritual mitzvahs. Of course, all Jews are ritually immersed at times for ritual cleansing, but not for John's searing admonition on repentance."

Nicodemus then said to me, "I now see what Jesus was all about. But back then, as you know and as Jesus correctly pointed out, I was not yet born again. Therefore, I could not understand what he was talking about. Back then I was a Torah-Observant Jew, and I therefore felt no need to repent. Repenting was for forgiveness, and I was sure I had no need for that."

I lifted my hand for Nicodemus to pause, and I said, "I am well aware of our Jewish, three-fold sin management system, my friend. We thought being right with God came from exercising scrupulous behavior, going to ritual purification baths when ceremonially unclean, and participating in the prescribed Temple offerings and sacrifices."

Nicodemus was animated now and interrupted me, saying, "Yes! It was our religious system that imputed righteousness, therefore I had no need to repent – and certainly not to be baptized. If anyone was righteous, it was me!"

He paused and looked at me with a pained expression. He was trying to form words, but his heart was so sad. So I replied, "I know, brother, I know. But Jesus made it immediately clear to you that even though you had a system for covering your sins, you were not fundamentally dealing with them. For that you would have to surrender all claim to any right to righteousness, and receive his grace … like a child receives a gift."

Nicodemus smiled and said, "That was the hardest part for me. Like a child? Me, the Important Teacher of Israel? But I just could not shrug off his words, John. They haunted me, and convicted me, and eventually I got down on my knees and surrendered my will and my life to him."

He paused for a moment, seemingly lost in his memories, and then said, "I knew there had to be something different about this young miracle-working rabbi. Even though I was deep into my career as a temple-observant Pharisee, and an important member of the Sanhedrin, I sensed there was something more. As soon as I witnessed Jesus around the temple grounds and listened to him teach and interact with the people, the Holy Spirit convicted me that I had to talk to him.

"And John, I am so grateful I did. Nothing was ever the same after my encounter with Jesus that night on the Mt of Olives. It was a defining moment in my life."

After the Passover Feast, we spent some time down near the Jordan. Jesus was teaching and the people were absolutely fascinated with him. They would often exclaim, "This man teaches as one who has authority, and not as our teachers of the law!"

Jesus would teach, and as the people's hearts were pierced, we would invite them down into the Jordan to be immersed. What a heady experience for us, his young disciples. What Jesus had said to us that day back on the beach was becoming a reality: we were becoming fishers of men.

But after a while Jesus was ready to head back to Galilee. He gathered us around him and said, "The Pharisees are missing the point of everything I am doing. They are talking about the fact that we are gaining and baptizing more disciples than John. I will never be seen as competing with my cousin. We are going to leave Judea and head back once more to Galilee."

We nodded, eager to follow him wherever he was going. As we were packing up our things he said, "I have to go through Samaria. I have an appointment at a well near Sychar. You have witnessed an encounter with Nicodemus, one of the "up and in," the rich and famous – a wealthy man with everything this world can provide." He paused, and then said, "I see a woman at a well who is the "down and out," – the poor and infamous. She needs to hear the good news of the kingdom as much as Nicodemus did.

With this we set out for Samaria, a place we would have preferred to avoid.

17

SAMARITAN WOMAN AT THE WELL

John 4

We had left the Judean area rather abruptly, but Jesus, as always, was moving with his calm, relaxed pace. He had a pace, and he had a purpose. He was not in constant motion, but he was always purposeful in his movement. We too often mistake motion, action, and activities for meaningful movement. His movement was always towards a purpose, and apparently he had a distinct purpose in mind for our trek into Samaria.

As we walked the forty or so miles into the Samaritan territory our minds were bouncing around, wondering just why our rabbi was so determined to take us through the middle of Samaria. Peter was murmuring to James about the unnecessary risk this involved, and Philip and Nathanael were whispering back and forth trying to guess our next destination.

I heard Thomas ask Judas, "What do you think he meant by, "I see a woman at a well who is the "down and out?" Judas shrugged his shoulders, and said, "I don't know. But I see no reason for us to be going through Samaria."

As you may know, we Jews did not get along well with the Samaritans. There was much bad blood, having built over many years. The Samaritans resented the Jews for their attitude of superiority. You see, this area of Jerusalem, between our Galilee in the upper north and the Judean region around Jerusalem towards the south, had been overrun during the first Assyrian conquest. The Assyrians' methodology was to mix up the cultures in their captured areas by relocating and intermarrying disparate peoples.

They carried many of the Jews off to other lands and introduced other ethnicities into Samaria. As these different races and cultures intermarried, any semblance of a pure Jewish culture eventually disappeared. It was a devastatingly effective way of dominating their victims.

Since that time, the Jews have looked down on the Samaritans, and the Samaritans have carried great resentment because of this condescending, superior attitude. Here is a quick summary of the bad blood history between the Jews and the Samaritans, so you may have a better understanding of the incredulity of Jesus' next encounter.

Around the year 538 before Jesus, Cyrus of Persia gave permission to and even encouraged the Jews in exile to return to Jerusalem. As the exiles were returning the Samaritans stood ready to welcome them back, and even to assist in the rebuilding of the temple. But the Jewish exiles rejected their open arms, and worse, rejected outright the Samaritans' offer to help with the temple. The exiles' disgust for the Samaritans was obvious and it was blatant.

This caused great animosity among the Samaritans, so they began to actively oppose the rebuilding of the temple, undermining the Jews' efforts among the Persian rulers. This slowed considerably the rebuilding efforts. You can read all about this in our books of Ezra and Nehemiah.

When the Samaritans built their temple on Mount Gerizim, precisely where our next stop would be, by the way, the break with Jerusalem was complete. But not the hostilities. The Samaritans assisted the Greek Seleucids against the Jews in the

Maccabean revolt around the year 167 before Jesus. The Jews then ravaged the Samaritan's temple around the beginning of the first century before Jesus. And the final insult was when the Samaritans scattered the bones of the dead in our temple in Jerusalem.

As you can see, the enmity, disdain, and outright hatred of the two groups ran deep. So, even though Galilean Jews, at times, took the direct route through Samaria on their journey to and from Jerusalem, most preferred the longer journey along the King's Highway, across the Jordan River in the Transjordan region. We were not at all comfortable with the Master's travel intentions. There was something about his pace and his purpose that was disturbing each of us, even if we could not put our fingers on it.

You will recall I said earlier that Jesus' encounter and conversation with Nicodemus while we were in Jerusalem, and then this next encounter with the Samaritan women at the well in Samaria, might possibly represent God's entire scriptural story. This is a bold and broad-sweeping declaration, I know. In both encounters Jesus is clearly about restoring, redeeming and reconciling God's people.

Therefore, as I said earlier, we will spend more time examining the teaching lessons to be found in these two encounters than we will, perhaps, in all the other encounters combined.

NOON AT THE WELL

We spent our first night outside the village of Ofra, near the top of Mt Baal-Hazor. This is close to where Absalom held the feast of sheep-shearing when Amnon was assassinated. You can read about this in our second book of the prophet Samuel. It is also the highest mountain around. We had not traveled far that first day, but Jesus wanted to climb back up to the road that runs atop the ridge between Jerusalem and Samaria before we stopped for the night.

After climbing the three thousand feet up from the Jordan river we were all fatigued. We gathered sticks together and built a fire, and we shared a meal of bread and figs and dates. After that we went straight to sleep. My eyes were heavy as I laid my head down to the crackling of the fire. The next morning we were up before dawn and on our way again. We were all happy to be moving on, but a little wary as we walked deeper into the Samarian region.

Peter was telling stories about his fishing exploits, and big brother James seemed determined to out-exaggerate him. Andrew and I walked together with Jesus for most of the morning, just enjoying his company. And to be sure, he enjoyed ours, as well. I think some of his best times were times like this, walking and talking. He loved nature and the outdoors, and would frequently stop and look out over the countryside, spreading his arms out wide and exclaiming something like our 19th Psalm:

"The heavens declare the glory of God;
  the skies proclaim the work of his hands.
Day after day they pour forth speech;
  night after night they reveal knowledge."

We were moving at a faster pace than normal, and after a few hours we came to a town in Samaria called Sychar, near the plot of ground Jacob had given to his son Joseph. Jacob's well was there, and Jesus, tired as he was from the journey, sat down by the well. This well has been here for almost two thousand years. So much history has taken place here. Yet a new kind of history was about to take place. A new history about his story.

It was about noon. The sun was up and in full force. We were all a little tired, but Jesus seemed unusually so. He directed us to go into the small town nearby to buy more food. Brother James pulled me aside and said, "The Master seems exhausted. I am worried about him. You follow us a little way, but then stay back just to be sure he is okay." He then frowned and said, "But do not make a nuisance of yourself."

I was irritated with James for treating me like a little brother, so I rolled my eyes at him. But to be honest it felt good to be given this responsibility. We all set off towards town, but after a short walk I stopped and circled back around and sat down against a big rock. The shade of the rock was a relief, so I stayed where I was – close enough to see and hear Jesus, but just barely.

I might have dosed a bit, but I heard a noise and looked up and saw a woman from the village walking up to the well. I was surprised to see a woman walking alone; this is just not something done in our culture. And it was midday when absolutely no one comes out to a well in the heat of the day. And, typically all the women come out together.

She looked downtrodden and weary. And I do not mean from the walk and the heat; she seemed as though life had beaten her down. Her shoulders were drooped, and she walked with a wandering pace, her eyes fixed on the ground. She was not unattractive, but her entire defeated demeanor cast her in an unfavorable light.

My first thought was, "She must have a horrible husband." She looked so dejected and downtrodden. Beaten up by life.

I watched as she approached Jesus, curious to see how a Samaritan woman would react to a Jewish man, and even vice-versa. Jesus was sitting on the side of the stone well but stood up as the woman drew near. He did not hesitate or even extend a greeting, other than to smile his usual warm, inviting smile. Before the woman could say a word Jesus said, "Will you give me a drink?"

I was as surprised by the Master's request as the woman obviously was. Her face registered suspicion initially, and she stepped back slightly. She slowly lowered her water jar and stood still. Her eyes narrowed as she said to him, "You are a Jew and I am a Samaritan woman. How can you ask me for a drink?"

She knew, and I knew, and of course Jesus knew, that Jews do not associate with Samaritans. But in Jesus' world of the Kingdom among us, this was immaterial. Apparently, he was intent on obliterating any such social roadblocks. For a Jewish man to talk with another Jewish woman in public, much less a Samaritan woman, without her husband no less, is just not allowed socially. For Jesus to strike up a conversation with a single, Samaritan, woman - in the middle of the day – is just unheard of!

But of course the Master knew exactly what he was doing. He was in the process of masterfully drawing in this down-and-out woman. He was going to establish common ground with her, put her at ease, and then begin to redeem, rescue and restore her.

Can you see, that by asking her for help, Jesus was eliminating any sense of superiority over her? Instead of powering up, as no doubt most of the men in her life had done, he powered down. Asking her for a drink, in essence asking for help, put him on her level. Because he was the absolute master at the intricacies of the heart, and of relationships, he knew this woman needed someone to meet her where she was. She had been beaten up enough by life, and by men, as we would soon find out.

If she had been kneeling down, or even lying down, I think Jesus would have gotten down on her level. Jesus had to begin by removing the barrier of rejection and the superiority of men, and specifically of a Jewish man. She needed connection, and Jesus was masterfully connecting with her. He regarded her for a moment, and then said,

> "If you knew the gift of God and who it is that asks you for a drink, you would have asked him, and he would have given you living water."

Living water is moving water. In our culture and religion, only moving water can be used for ritual cleansing. Our Mikveh ritual cleansing baths are designed to have moving water, so that when we immerse ourselves, we are ritually clean. The moving water "takes away our sin." Jesus would often use such examples from our everyday life to capture our attention. But like Nicodemus, this woman was not yet following Jesus' deeper meaning.

The living water is Kingdom living water! Not the dreary water of religion. Not the tired and ineffective water of sin management or religious performance. No, Jesus had living water for this woman, and she would soon understand what he meant. But for now she was still operating, much like Nicodemus before, on the ground level of his literal meaning, and missing the deeper spiritual message.

THE WELL IS DEEP

The woman – we later discovered her name was Ma'im (Hebrew for water) - pulled her hair back from her forehead and wiped a bead of sweat from her eyes. "Sir," Ma'im said, sitting down beside the well, "you have nothing to draw with and the well is deep. Where can you get this living water?"

As she said this she looked down into the well, and then looked up at Jesus. Her eyes went to his hands, where he obviously was not holding a bucket of any sort. She was thinking, as perhaps you do when things appear hopeless, or problems seem insurmountable, that Jesus has nothing with which to help her, in her situation.

Perhaps the well of your hurt is deep, like Ma'im's well of hurt. The years of rejection, or failure, or missteps, bad decisions, or just plain bad luck have deepened the well to the point you have no ability and no hope to find living water. Either you made bad decisions, or someone else hurt you, but regardless, you feel as though nothing but dead or dying water is flowing through your life.

Or, you might say that any experience you have had with religion has been a far cry from any dynamic, living water. This would be the plight of Ma'im. She was truly down and out. Life and religion had left her parched.

But perhaps you are not as desperate as she. Your problems are circumstantial, not life-long. They are still very real to you, but you are not as beaten down by life as this woman. But! - you may still think the well of your current problem, or pain is too deep for Jesus. You may still assume he just does not have a bucket for your issue. In your prayers you halfheartedly ask him for living water, healing water, or even fixing water, but in your heart, you do not believe he has a rope and bucket to reach the depth of your challenge.

He does, my friend, he does.

I watched Ma'im as her eyes dropped and she stared into the deepness of the well. She was lost in thought. Jesus let her work through her emotions, saying nothing. A bird of prey flew overhead, calling out after its victims. She looked up at the bird for a moment, deep in thought. Perhaps she was thinking she was indeed a victim herself.

Jesus pointed down into the well and looked into her eyes. He smiled softly and said, "If you drink from Jacob's well you'll be thirsty again and again, but if anyone drinks the living water I give them, they will never thirst again and will be forever satisfied! For when you drink the water I give you, it becomes a gushing fountain of the Holy Spirit, springing up and flooding you with endless life!"

She laughed a quiet laugh; she scoffed, actually, with a smirk on her face. She knew she was thirsty for another life, but she did not think another life was possible. Not now, not in her situation. Not after all the mistakes she had made. Always thirsting for a better life was all she knew.

Later, when we were in Jerusalem for the Feast of Tabernacles, Jesus stood up on the last and greatest day of the feast and exclaimed something very similar:

> "All you thirsty ones, come to me! Come to me and drink! Believe in me so that rivers of living water will burst out from within you, flowing from your

> innermost being, just like the Scripture says." Whoever surrenders and puts their trust in me rivers of living water will flow from within them."

By this he meant the Spirit, whom those who believed in him were later to receive. Up to that time the Spirit had not been given, since Jesus had not yet been glorified.

Water is such a crucial aspect to our lives in Israel. We are surrounded by so much desert, and our climate has only a short rainy season. In our forty-second psalm, the psalmist was speaking directly to this woman. Perhaps to you, too?

> As the deer pants for streams of water,
> so my soul pants for you, my God.
> My soul thirsts for God, for the living God.
> When can I go and meet with God?
> My tears have been my food
> day and night,
> while people say to me all day long,
> "Where is your God?"
>
> My soul is downcast within me;
> therefore I will remember you
> from the land of the Jordan,
> the heights of Hermon—from Mount Mizar.
> Deep calls to deep
> in the roar of your waterfalls;
> all your waves and breakers
> have swept over me.

Considering Jesus' emphasis on living water, let us pause for a moment and think about this image of living water welling up and overflowing with eternal ... *Life.*

18

DARK HOLES

John 4

At the beginning of our story I wrote, "In him was life, and that life was the light of all mankind. The light shines in the darkness, and the darkness has not understood it nor overcome it."

Jesus was bringing his Light and his Life to Ma'im . He was not interested in just fixing her problems; he was intent on rescuing, redeeming and restoring her to be a child of God. He was going to rescue her and redeem her into God's Family. A new child overflowing with Living Water. Ma'im was filled with holes – holes of defeat, holes of loneliness, holes of desire, and especially holes of intimacy. She had tried to fill her holes with men, but of course to no avail. Dead water had drained the life out of her.

We, too, try to fill our holes with social and cultural water, which never satisfies and never fills us. And so, as Jesus said, we are continually thirsty for something real, true, and lasting. Until we meet Jesus, and allow him to fill up all our holes, we are back again and again, often to the same old tired wells, which can never satisfy, desperate for a taste of living water.

We just do not know where to find it. And we are searching in all the wrong places.

In a similar fashion, during our last night together before Jesus was arrested, he told us this, "Peace I leave with you; my peace I give you. I do not give to you as the world gives."

"Not as the world gives." The world's peace will never give you peace, just as the world's water will never satisfy your thirst. If we knew the gift of God, we would ask him, and he would give us the living water of true peace.

Jesus does not just fill all our holes, although that would be miracle enough. No, he fills us to the point of overflowing. He is no stopgap, thirst-quencher; he satisfies and then eliminates our thirst altogether. That thirst we have been trying to quench all our lives with things, activities and relationships diminishes and then disappears when we surrender our lives to Jesus - and seek him, and only him to fill the holes which we all have.

Can you imagine the freedom in that!

Are you filling up on Jesus' living water? Or are the holes still within you draining out any hope of his true Life to the full?

I watched as Ma'im tried to understand what Jesus was saying about this spring of Living Water. She opened her mouth to speak then closed it. I could not read her mind, but she was obviously wrestling with what to say next. After a moment her shoulders drooped, in a sign of defeat and discouragement, and she said to him, "Sir, give me this water so that I won't get thirsty and have to keep coming here to draw water."

Is this not the cry of all of us; the cry of the world; the cry of all the lost people stumbling around in the darkness, trying to find some meaning and purpose in their lives? Their thirst for peace is never quenched; their hunger for joy is never sated. This woman did not realize her deepest need was Jesus – not water. But by the grace of God, she was about to find out.

At this point I could see my fellow disciples coming up the path from the village. They were still a way off, but perhaps Jesus sensed their approach, so he shifted course and abruptly said to her, "Go, call your husband and come back."

"I have no husband," she replied, her whole body deflating. Ma'im let out a sigh as her chest rose and then fell. She was fighting to stay in control. It was as though her sheer essence shrunk, her entire being collapsing inward, like a wineskin emptying out. She looked at this man, trying to understand who, or what, he was. She then looked away, back towards the village, tears forming in her eyes.

Jesus said to her, "You are right when you say you have no husband. The fact is, you have had five husbands, and the man you now have is not your husband. What you have just said is quite true."

I was somewhat taken aback by Jesus' blunt response. He seemed to have shifted from soft grace to blunt truth. What was he doing? And how did he know about her five husbands? I sat up and leaned forward to hear what would come next.

"Sir," Ma'im said, clearly exasperated, "I can see that you are a prophet. Our ancestors worshiped on this mountain, but you Jews claim that the place where we must worship is in Jerusalem. What do you say to that? Are you Jews right, or are we?"

The mountain to which she was referring is Mt. Gerizim, and as I said before, it is where the Samaritans built their own temple, which the Jews attacked.

She now realized this man before her was a prophet of some sort. Jesus had her rapt attention and was not going to entertain even a discussion of these old diversions of contention and religious debate. As with Nicodemus, he was aiming much deeper.

SPIRIT AND TRUTH

"Woman," Jesus replied, standing up, "believe me, a time is coming when you will worship the Father neither on this mountain nor in Jerusalem. A time is coming and has now come when the true worshipers will worship the Father in the Spirit and in truth, for they are the kind of worshipers the Father seeks. God is spirit, and his worshipers must worship in the Spirit and in truth."

May I take a moment to dive a little deeper into this clarion call to worship: "in Spirit and in truth?" I believe this is the missing link for so many well-meaning, sincere, but sincerely wrong religious people. They are seeking to worship God, but they are falling into Satan's diversionary trap of the non-essentials.

It is not where you worship, but who you worship. It is not how you worship, but if you worship with the Spirit who indwells you. It is not a matter of the right place, but of the right heart. You are, after all, the temple, now that the Holy Spirit indwells you. Paul spoke succinctly of this in his first letter to the Family in Corinth. He first told the Family of Followers they, as a family, are the temple:

> Don't you know that you yourselves are God's temple and that God's Spirit dwells in your midst?

He then told them that their individual bodies are the temple:

> Do you not know that your bodies are temples of the Holy Spirit, who is in you, whom you have received from God?

And now we have circled back around to my opening statement, as I introduced these two encounters with Nicodemus and this Samaritan woman. Jesus' entire overarching message is captured in these two encounters:

You must be born again by and with the Holy Spirit.

You must worship with and through this same Holy Spirit.

The truth, the only truth, is found through the Holy Spirit. He would later tell us the Spirit will always guide us into all truth. He even told us,

> "I am the way, the truth and the life. If you hold to my teaching, you are really my disciples. Then you will know the truth, and the truth will set you free."

Jesus is telling this woman at the well, and he is telling you, that your once-a-week, praise songs, or going to Fellowship meetings, or to synagogue, may not be true worship at all. True worship is not about singing, praising and praying, although it can certainly include any and all of these. True worship is about connecting with the Truth through the Spirit of Truth.

True worship is about surrendering. Our Aramaic word for worship, *seged,* means *to bow down,* but also *to surrender.* Surrender is the key that unlocks the door to salvation. When we truly surrender to Jesus we are born again, and the Holy Spirit immediately indwells us. Surrender is therefore the key that opens the door to true worship, to worship in Spirit and in truth. Only a surrendered heart can truly worship because only a surrendered heart will bow down. Not a negotiated surrender, mind you, a full-out total surrender of my way and my will.

Jesus made it clear to us we could worship anytime, anywhere, if we have the Spirit, and if we seek him through the Spirit. In this way we would always find the truth, and that truth would set us free. As we live and breathe and have our being in him, in an everyday conversational walk through life with him, talking about what we are doing together, we are worshipping him in Spirit and in truth.

19

THE FIRST EVANGELIST

John 4

Ma'im stood up from the well, wiped her sweaty brow, shrugged and said, "I know that Messiah (called Christ) is coming. When he comes, he will explain everything to us." She shielded her eyes against the glaring sun, or against Jesus' penetrating eyes, I am not sure which. She stared at Jesus, daring him to say more.

Jesus looked at her intently. He hesitated for a moment, letting the silence fill the air. Looking back on this, I wonder if he was waiting for the Spirit to give him the go-ahead to reveal his true identity. He then declared, in a confident, but soft voice, "I am the *I Am* who speaks to you—I am he, the Messiah you have been waiting for."

There was a moment, a hesitation, a look between Jesus and Ma'im. I saw it and felt a stirring in my soul. There was some kind of communication going on, but not with words. It was deep calling unto deep.

I was astonished to hear Jesus make this declaration about himself to this woman. He was stating for the first time - the first time! - that he is indeed the long-awaited Messiah! And at this

Samaritan village well, away from any crowds, away even from his disciples. Why had he chosen this place? To understand this, we must revisit the stories of the Patriarchs.

Jesus later reminded us that this was not just any well. This is the place called Shechem in the stories of our patriarchs, in a grassy area nestled between the two mountains, Mt Gerizim and Mt Ebal. In our book of Beginnings, called Genesis in the Septuagint, Abraham stopped here on his journey from Haran to the Promised Land:

> So Abram went, as the LORD had told him; and Lot went with him. Abram was seventy-five years old when he set out from Harran. He took his wife Sarai, his nephew Lot, all the possessions they had accumulated and the people they had acquired in Harran, and they set out for the land of Canaan, and they arrived there.
>
> Abram traveled through the land as far as the site of the great tree of Moreh at Shechem. At that time the Canaanites were in the land. The LORD appeared to Abram and said, "To your offspring I will give this land." So he built an altar there to the LORD, who had appeared to him. (Genesis 12:4-6)

And, after reconciling with his brother Esau, Jacob settled here:

> So that day Esau started on his way back to Seir. Jacob, however, went to Sukkoth, where he built a place for himself and made shelters for his livestock. That is why the place is called Sukkoth.
>
> After Jacob came from Paddan Aram, he arrived safely at the city of Shechem in Canaan and camped within sight of the city. For a hundred pieces of silver, he bought from the sons of Hamor, the father of

> Shechem, the plot of ground where he pitched his tent. There he set up an altar and called it El Elohe Israel.

Joseph's brothers were grazing the flocks near Shechem when Joseph was sent by his father Jacob to check on them. Even Joseph's bones are buried here.

No, this is no random area Jesus has chosen to meet this woman. As with so many of our stories, everything is tied to the land and its rich history. And it is here Jesus chose to declare his true identity as the long-awaited Messiah.

But to a lowly, insignificant Samaritan woman – or seemingly insignificant? Of course, there is simply no such lowly person in Jesus' world, and no one, not one person is insignificant. One person, each person, matters immensely to God the Father, and therefore to Jesus. I could hardly process what I was hearing. Then I heard the other disciples chatting among themselves as they returned from the village. They were surprised to find Jesus talking with a woman. But no one asked, "What do you want?" or "Why are you talking with her?"

I joined the group, and suddenly Ma'im left her water jar and hurried back to the town. She had a new energy. Her shoulders were no longer drooping. Her countenance was positive and purposeful. Leaving her jar meant she was either startled by the return of this group of Jewish men, or she planned to come right back. Or both. Or … perhaps her initial reason for coming to the well was no longer important.

Jesus glanced over my way, winked, and said, "Did you enjoy your nap behind the rock?" My face colored in embarrassment, but I knew he was just teasing me.

HOLY SPIRIT ENERGY

Meanwhile, Peter and James urged him, "Rabbi, eat something." They laid out some bread and dates and figs, along with some goat's milk they had purchased from the villagers. But Jesus said to them, "I have food to eat that you know nothing about." Then my brother James asked me, "Did that woman bring him food?"

I was about to answer when Jesus interrupted me and said, "My food is to do the will of him who sent me and to finish his work."

Food is for energy, and Jesus was telling us he was energized by his mission to rescue and redeem and restore the lost children of Israel. I could see this energy rising in him as he interacted with Ma'im. He lived and breathed to seek and save the lost. It was his manna, his heaven-sent sustenance.

Often, when he was surrounded by the sick and the lost, he would lose track of time and go for hours without eating or even resting. Once his mother and brothers tried to "rescue" him from himself. John Mark recorded this in his Gospel:

> When Jesus entered a house, and again a crowd gathered, so that he and his disciples were not even able to eat. When his family heard about this, they went to take charge of him, for they said, "He is out of his mind."

He was not out of his mind on that occasion, and no one had brought him food on this occasion. He was precisely in his right mind, doing his Father's will, and therefore everything else, including food and rest, could wait.

I have learned what Jesus meant by the energy and sustenance that comes from doing the will of the Father. It is so energizing to watch the Holy Spirit move in someone's life. To be there, when someone can suddenly see for the first time – with spiritual eyes – with the eyes of their heart enlightened. I could go days without eating when that kind of Holy Spirit energy is surging.

At this point the villagers, led by Ma'im, were walking at a fast pace out to see us. She was animated, urging the villagers on.

I could not tell if they were friend or foe, but Jesus was not distracted in the least by their approach. He pointed to the crowd, still off in the distance, then looked back at our group and said, "Don't you have a saying, 'It's still four months until harvest'?"

We nodded, confused, waiting for him to explain. We were obviously confused, so he pointed again at the crowd and said, "I tell you, open your eyes and look at the fields! They are ripe for harvest. Even now the one who reaps draws a wage and harvests a crop for eternal life, so that the sower and the reaper may be glad together. Thus the saying 'One sows and another reaps' is true."

Little did we know Ma'im had rushed back into the village, gathering everyone she could find around her, and exclaimed to the people, "Come, see a man who told me everything I ever did. (She seemed to have lost all shame over 'everything she did.') Could this be the Messiah?" she exclaimed excitedly. So they came out of the town and made their way toward us, led by a woman to whom they would not even have acknowledged just a few hours earlier.

I love the Father's way of doing things.

Many of the Samaritans from that town initially believed in Jesus because of Ma'im 's testimony, "He told me everything I ever did." But as they gathered around Jesus he began to teach them, telling them all about the good news of the Kingdom of God. They were taken aback by his willingness, as a Jewish rabbi, to interact with them, and equally taken aback by the authority with which he taught.

They, as so many others, remarked, "He does not teach like anyone we have ever heard! Our teachers quote other rabbis and teachers and prophets. But this man speaks as if he is *the authority*, and he is *the source,* for all those who came before him." So they urged him to stay with them, and we did. And because of his words many more became believers. I overheard them say to Ma'im, "We no longer believe just because of what you said; now we have heard for ourselves."

We spent two days in that village. They fed us well and provided comfortable sleeping arrangements for us all. Ma'im was a new woman – rescued and redeemed. Jesus had sought her out to restore her, and restore her he did. We never met the man she was living with prior to this, and my guess is he was ashamed to show his face, now that she was a restored member of the community. We learned a lesson that day. A lesson Jesus would show us many times by his actions and his words:

> In Christ Jesus we are all children of God through faith, for all of us who were baptized into Christ have clothed ourselves with Christ. There is neither Jew nor Gentile, neither slave nor free, nor is there male and female, nor Samaritan, for all are one in Christ Jesus. If we belong to Christ, then we are Abraham's seed, and heirs according to the promise.

After the two days we left for Galilee, not knowing if we would see these Samaritans again, but knowing we would celebrate with them one day in the renewal of all things. Much later I realized this woman was the first evangelist to win a city to Jesus!

20

EVANGELISM IS AS SIMPLE AS 1-2-3

"I tell you, open your eyes and look at the fields!" Jesus had told us. "They are ripe for harvest. Even now the one who reaps draws a wage and harvests a crop for eternal life, so that the sower and the reaper may be glad together. Thus the saying 'One sows and another reaps' is true. I sent you to reap what you have not worked for. Others have done the hard work, and you have reaped the benefits of their labor."

I have reflected many times on the comparison and the contrast between Jesus' interaction with Nicodemus and this Samaritan woman. With Nicodemus, a learned man of the upper crust of society, Jesus went straight for the truth. He knew Nicodemus needed truth first and grace second. But with Ma'im, an unlearned woman of the lower edges of society, he knew she needed to be overwhelmed with grace first, before he presented *truth* to her.

Jesus was the master evangelist. He understood the deepest needs of everyone he encountered, and he related to them according to their individual needs. What I learned watching Jesus, and through trial and error over the years, is that evangelism is as simple as 1-2-3:

1. One Person: Matters to God
2. Two Principles: Evangelism is a process and God is responsible for the results
3. Three Barriers: Emotional, Intellectual and Volitional.

ONE PERSON MATTERS TO GOD

Jesus is not asking you to preach to the masses, but instead to reach that one person he puts in your path. Just like this Samaritan woman. Reach, not preach, mind you.

This Samaritan woman, this one person, seems so insignificant in the big scheme of things. Yet Jesus purposely sought her out. Ma'im was important to him, and she, or someone like her, should be just as important to you. Not only was she not insignificant, she became the first female evangelist to win a city to Jesus! Who would have known?

Jesus.

GRACE AND TRUTH

The proper relationship between grace and truth is so critically important to understand when reaching out to people. As I concluded my introduction earlier:

> The Word became flesh and made his dwelling among us. We have seen his glory, the glory of the one and only Son, who came from the Father, *full of grace and truth.*

Grace and truth – the order of these are so important, and Jesus demonstrated this in the way he interacted with so many of those who were in dire need of grace, as was this woman at the well. Therefore, let your conversations be always full of grace, seasoned with salt (truth).

My mother, Salome, made a wonderful stew. You should have seen me devouring it, or perhaps you shouldn't. James would laugh and say, "Why don't you just tie on the feed bag, little brother? You look like a donkey at the trough with your bowl turned up to your mouth!"

Oh, it was so delicious. She seasoned it perfectly with just the right touch of salt. But think about this: if my mother added no salt, the stew would be bland. But if she added too much salt, the stew would be too strong, too bitter, and no one would enjoy eating it.

So it is with how we deal with others. The stew is the grace. The salt is the truth. Let your conversations be full of grace, yet seasoned with the truth. If we overwhelm someone with truth first, i.e., too much salt, they typically will not be able to receive our message, and they certainly will not see Jesus in us.

Be always full of grace, first, as was the Master.

TWO IMPORTANT PRINCIPLES

I hope you can see by now that evangelism is a process and God is responsible for the results, not you.

Not you!

Over all these years of introducing the lost to Jesus, and watching others do the same, I have seen problems arise when we think evangelism is an event rather than a process. We somehow feel it is up to us to convince them to surrender their hearts to Jesus and be saved. So we press and push them, and the result is stress, for both parties. But if we understand that God is responsible for the results, and we certainly are not, we can relax and enjoy the process.

Jesus modeled this process by gaining common ground with Ma'im. He first asked her for a drink. He then engaged her in an ongoing conversation (grace) long before he brought up her marriage situation (truth).

The process of evangelism involves us establishing common ground, and then planting seeds of grace and truth. I can plant seeds. You can plant seeds. Anyone can and everyone should plant seeds of grace and truth. These simple governing principles of evangelism are captured perfectly in Paul's first letter to the Followers in Corinth:

> What, after all, is Apollos? And what is Paul? Only servants, through whom you came to believe—as the Lord has assigned to each his task.
>
> I planted the seed, Apollos watered it, but God has been making it grow.
>
> So neither the one who plants nor the one who waters is anything, but only God, who makes things grow. The one who plants and the one who waters have one purpose, and they will each be rewarded according to their own labor. For we are God's fellow workers; you are God's field, God's building.

At times we plant seeds of grace and sometimes we water where someone else has already planted, but it is God who makes them grow. Not us. So relax, be purposeful, and spread the seeds of the joy of Jesus to those around you.

THREE BARRIERS

Most people I encounter have one or more of these three barriers:

The Emotional Barrier: They have had a bad experience with religion and/or religious people.

The Intellectual Barrier: They have bad information about our scriptures, God, and/or what it means to follow Jesus.

The Volitional Barrier: They have a bad will – or more accurately, a stubborn heart. This does not mean they are necessarily bad people, but their heart is hardened, due to pride and to Self.

Clearly Ma'im had emotional barriers. She had erected rock-solid barriers to protect her heart. She had no doubt experienced boorish and condescending behavior from "God's chosen people." She had obviously experienced bad behavior by men: five divorces and now living with a man who does not respect her, or care enough for her to marry her.

Ma'im desperately needed to have her bad experiences replaced with good experiences. Which is precisely what Jesus did. Unlike Nicodemus, she did not need good information first and foremost, although Jesus eventually did correct her bad information. She needed a good experience.

So, for those with emotional barriers we replace bad experiences with good experiences. We let them see our joy. We let them feel our love and our compassion for them. We share our stew of grace with them. We show them that Jesus is never about condemnation. We show them Jesus loves them unconditionally, and do not miss this: that he actually likes them, too. We let them see that Jesus can be our best friend.

For the Intellectual Barrier, we replace bad information with good information. Many people I encounter think the scriptures are all about restrictive rules and performance. And there are many other mistaken ideas about following Jesus, as well. Nicodemus was hung up on performance. Ma'im was hung up on where to worship.

We want to be ready to replace their bad information with good information – or ready to take them to someone who can. As my dear friend Peter said in his first letter,

> Always be prepared to give an answer to everyone who asks you to give the reason for the hope that you have. *But do this with gentleness and respect.*

Now for those with a Volitional Barrier, a hardened heart, we must simply pray for them. The rich young ruler had a hard heart. (You recall the story of this wealthy young man asking Jesus what good thing he could do to guarantee his way to Heaven? Jesus told him to sell all his possessions, which he would not do.) He was a good man, but his stubborn heart was not ready to surrender to Jesus. I remember several times Jesus praying for that young man. He prayed the Holy Spirit would soften his heart and open his eyes to the truth.

So we follow the Master's lead and continue to lift those stubborn hearts up to the Father. The Holy Spirit can break their hard outer shell in the most perfect of ways. Sometimes with a hammer, and sometimes with his heart.

To conclude, my friend, plant seeds, water seeds, and be ready for God's harvest!

21

HE TOOK JESUS AT HIS WORD

John 5

After our two days with the Samaritans we left for Galilee. Now Jesus himself had pointed out that a prophet has no honor in his own country, but when we arrived in Galilee the people welcomed him. They had seen all that he had done in Jerusalem at the Passover Festival, for they also had been there.

For a few days James and I joined our father fishing. He was so proud of us. He kept saying, "My two sons – Talmidim (disciples) of this great new prophet and rabbi!" He would grin and pat us on the back, even hugging us. James did not especially like the hugging, but I did. Remember, every Jewish father's dream for his sons is that they become disciples of a rabbi. Abba was so proud that his boys were now disciples, and especially disciples of this new, exciting rabbi about whom everyone was talking.

It was good to be back with Abba, and good to be back fishing. The Sea of Galilee was our home, and I breathed in the fresh air and the beautiful scenery. I watched fish jumping out of the water and the sea birds filling the air. The sun was glimmering on the surface and the shimmering light lit up my heart. Galilee, the beautiful, lush, green rolling hills of my heart and home.

I wondered from time to time what would be our fate now that we were following Jesus. Would he lead our people in a rebellion over Rome and establish a new kingdom for Israel as the prophets had foreseen? If so, would we, his Talmidim, live in Jerusalem or here in Galilee? I am embarrassed to admit it, but I also wondered what my role would be in this new kingdom.

I realize you only know me as a seasoned, wise old man, filled with the Holy Spirit's power, and his love, joy, peace and patience. But I was not always this way. All spiritual growth is a process. In my early days following Jesus, I was clueless. So yes, I pondered how Jesus would utilize us in his new kingdom – and in particular how he would utilize me.

Oy Veh!

Peter and Andrew were fishing, too. Peter was glad to be back with his wife, Ruth, and to her cooking! While we were tending the nets together he would walk around holding his belly and exclaiming, "Boy am I getting fat off Ruth's fine cooking!"

Nathanael left to spend a few days with his family in Cana, and Philip joined his fishing friends in Bethsaida, just up the coast from us. But none of us could focus completely on our family or our fishing. We knew we had been called to follow this captivating new rabbi, so we worked, visited, and relaxed, but all the while waiting for Jesus' next move.

Soon enough Jesus came calling. He said he wanted to visit Cana again. He did not say why, and we had already learned not to ask, so we packed a few things and began the walk over to Nathanael's home. It was about twenty miles and most of it uphill. We made the walk in one day, arriving late, but in time for Nathanael's family to set out a meal for us.

We ate to our heart's content. Nathanael's mother had cooked a scrumptious meal of stew, delicious bread, with olive oil, dates, and vegetables. His father had invited several friends over to hear the visiting rabbi. Jesus was enjoying his time, and asking questions of the guests, maybe even more so than teaching. The wine was flowing and the food was delicious. The fellowship was warm and comfortable, and from time to time Peter would interject some story, and we would all laugh and roll our eyes. Jesus loved this time with family and friends. As the sun settled behind the Galilean hills, we each found a place to lay down and sleep.

The next day the family from the wedding - the one where Jesus had turned the water into wine - came by and invited us to a feast in Jesus' honor. By this time the water-to-wine miracle was practically folklore in Cana and the surrounding area, but they had also heard about the other miracles Jesus had been performing. The excitement in the air was palpable, and the joy was energizing.

The family left to prepare the feast, killing the fatted calf and organizing their servants' activities. As they left the father turned back, a huge smile on his face and said, "And trust me, Master, we will not run out of wine this time!" We all smiled, and Jesus burst out laughing. He so loved a good joke.

THE ROYAL OFFICIAL

Shortly after the family left us a royal official from Capernaum arrived. He worked for Herod Antipas and was well known in the Capernaum area. He was a good man and acted fairly towards the Jews, but some disliked him because he was working for the hated Herod.

He had several servants and guards with him as they came riding up on horses. The horses were sweating and snorting, having been ridden hard. Whatever the business of this official, he was in a hurry, and very stressed. Nathanael stepped over to help with his horse, but his companions stayed in their saddles.

I watched as he approached Jesus. There was no air of superiority about him. He was clearly desperate. The panicked look on his face said it all. He looked at Jesus, spread his arms out, and in anguish said, "My son is deathly sick back in Capernaum.

I have heard of your miracles, and when I was told you had arrived in Galilee from Judea I had to find you to beg you to come and heal my son who is so close to death."

Jesus' response startled me. He looked first at the man, then at the small crowd that had gathered around us, and said, "Unless you people see signs and wonders you will never believe."

Later he told us he was referring to the fact that so many were impressed with his miracles, but not who he is. He was frustrated that the people were focusing more on his actions and not his words. He was a teacher at heart, not a miracle worker. And he never did miracles just to show off or to impress people.

But the man was clearly desperate, and therefore ready to swallow his pride, so he pressed on with Jesus. He dropped to his knees, a surprising act of humility for a royal official, and he cried out, "Rabbi, come down before my child dies!"

There was a moment, a hesitation, a look between Jesus and this man. They held each other's gaze for a moment. I saw it and felt a stirring in my soul. There was some kind of communication going on, but not with words. It was deep calling unto deep.

After a moment Jesus nodded and said, "Go," pointing back towards Capernaum, "your son will live."

The man looked at Jesus for a moment, then he looked around at us. He turned towards his horse, but then stopped and looked back at Jesus. He opened his mouth to say something, then closed it. He then slowly turned and mounted his horse. He held Jesus' look for a moment, then nodded his head slightly, as did Jesus in return. He pulled the reins on his horse as he turned his head towards Capernaum and galloped off, his entourage following him in a cloud of dust.

He took Jesus at his word and departed. While he was still on the way, his servants met him with the news that his boy was living. When he inquired as to the time his son got better, they said to him, "Yesterday, at one in the afternoon, the fever left him."

Then the father realized that this was the exact time at which Jesus had said to him, "Your son will live." So, he and his whole household believed.

This was the second sign Jesus performed after coming from Judea to Galilee, and the first he performed at a distance. We had somehow rationalized his water-to-wine miracle as, well, not normal, but perhaps understandable in some sense, because he was physically there – in person. But to heal someone from a distance? Just to say the word, and a deathly ill young son miles away is healed – on the spot?

Who is this man?

This was new and unprecedented in our world. We talked about it among ourselves, wondering who this Jesus really was, and what might be coming next. Andrew was about to speak but Peter interrupted him and said, "Well, whoever he is, and I know some say John the Baptist, others say Elijah, and still others, Jeremiah, or one of the prophets, I can tell you that I am in. I am committed. I do not have to see any more miracles. Just being with Jesus is miracle enough. He has life; he speaks life; he overflows with life."

"Besides," Peter continued, "to whom shall we go? Jesus has the words of eternal life. I think we all agree we have now come to believe and to know that he is the Holy One of God."

We all nodded and looked around at each other. I then said, "Did you notice what the official did? He just took Jesus at his word and departed?" Nathanael replied, nodding his head enthusiastically. "You know, I was going to say something about that. His response made an impression on the Master. I watched him as the man left. His eyes had a curious glimmer. It was as if he was surprised that the man just took him at his word, with no follow up questions, no asking for a guarantee, no second-guessing Jesus."

James added, "Would it be that I had that kind of trust." He slowly shook his head and said, "I am afraid I would have stood around for a few moments, asking Jesus for some kind of assurance, or direction, or something. A sign or something to make me feel better. But he just turned around and left. He just simply took Jesus at this word."

Matthew stood up, paused for a moment (he was a most deliberative and thoughtful man), and said, "This is the second Gentile, and both from Capernaum, who has captured the Master's rapt attention by their extraordinary trust. Think about Jesus' response to the Roman Centurion:

> A centurion's servant, whom his master valued highly, was sick and about to die. The centurion heard of Jesus and sent some elders of the Jews to him, asking him to come and heal his servant. When they came to Jesus, they pleaded earnestly with him, "This man deserves to have you do this, [5] because he loves our nation and has built our synagogue." So Jesus went with them.
>
> He was not far from the house when the centurion sent friends to say to him: "Lord, don't trouble yourself, for I do not deserve to have you come under my roof. That is why I did not even consider myself worthy to come to you.
>
> But say the word, and my servant will be healed. For I myself am a man under authority, with soldiers under me. I tell this one, 'Go,' and he goes; and that one, 'Come,' and he comes. I say to my servant, 'Do this,' and he does it."
>
> When Jesus heard this, he was amazed at him, and turning to the crowd following him, he said, "I tell you, I have not found such great faith even in Israel."

Andrew nodded and said, "I know, it reminded me immediately of our father Abraham, and his response to Yahweh when he took him outside and said,

> "Look up at the sky and count the stars—if indeed you can count them." Then he said to him, "So shall your offspring be.' And Abram believed the LORD, and he credited it to him as righteousness."

Andrew continued, "It is as if the royal official, like Abraham, trusted God and just totally abandoned the outcome of his beloved son to Jesus."

22

ABANDON THE OUTCOME TO GOD

I must pause for us to ponder this idea for a moment: Abandoning the outcome to God. Is this something you think you could do? What kind of trust would it take to be able to live this way? To take Jesus at his word and walk away from trying to control the outcome? It would take the kind of trust Jesus would want you to have. Not just to believe in Jesus, but believe what he said, no matter how counterintuitive. This is the kind of trust the Master would want you to have.

I have learned that even though Jesus understood our human weaknesses, it still perplexed him at times that we did not fully trust him, especially after witnessing his miracles. He even said this to a group of Jews in the midst of a debate with them over who he was:

> "Do not believe me unless I do the works of my Father. But if I do them, even though you do not believe me, believe the works, that you may know and understand that the Father is in me, and I in the Father."

And on our last night with him, after Philip had said, "Lord, show us the Father and that will be enough for us," Jesus had answered:

> "Don't you know me, Philip, even after I have been among you such a long time? Anyone who has seen me has seen the Father. How can you say, 'Show us the Father'? Don't you believe that I am in the Father, and that the Father is in me?"

I think many of us believe in Jesus, but we do not yet believe what Jesus believed.

Jesus graciously forgives our many setbacks, stumbles and sins, but he will not accept our desire for a compromise. He wants us to abandon ourselves to him. Abandon our lives to him. What we want is a "negotiated surrender" to Jesus. We want a compromise, which simply is our attempt to hold onto Self, and our agenda – and even some of our pet sins. We want to hold onto Self, and the outcomes we desire, while adding "a little Jesus" to our lives.

I used to be that way early on. I wanted a balance of some of me and some of him. I thought that would be a good balance. But all that produces is a lukewarm follower of Jesus, and he is not interested in lukewarm.

My dear child, as we learn to trust Jesus we can loosen our grip on the people and things around us, and learn to live more freely and lightly. If you want to live Jesus' "life to the full" you must learn to do this. You must! It is the key to the life that is truly life. When you learn to take your hands off the outcome, to loosen your grip, to stop trying to control the outcome, God's grace and peace will indeed be poured out on you and through you abundantly.

You will overflow with grace and peace and freedom. You will sense it, you will see it, and trust me, those around you will sense it and see it, too. They will praise Jesus for such an astounding miracle done in you, especially if you had been a controlling person. When you relax your grip, Jesus' peace will begin to flow in you and through you, and soon enough it will flow out of you, onto, and even into those around you.

This is in part what Jesus meant when he said,

> "Streams of living water will flow from within you."

ABANDON

But you must learn to abandon the outcome to Jesus. I could say, "Learn to let go of the outcome," but *abandon* has more gravitas, more finality. Abandon carries a sense of total release, as in, "I am turning my back and walking away from the outcome."

Think about this for a moment. If you heard that a man had left his wife and children, you would form one image in your mind. But if you heard he had abandoned his wife and children, an entirely different image forms. If a shepherd left his flock to pursue a missing sheep, you would understand. But if you heard he abandoned his flock, well, we both know this would be entirely unacceptable.

If you were to say, "I left my former way of life to follow Jesus," that would be admirable. But if you declared unequivocally, "I have abandoned my old life for Jesus," that would be astounding. Abandoning is the operative word. It is what Jesus meant when he said,

> "If anyone comes to me and does not hate – put in second place - father and mother, wife and children, brothers and sisters—yes, even their own life—such a person cannot be my disciple. And whoever does not carry their cross and follow me cannot be my disciple."

Abandoning the outcome to Jesus is the only practical thing to do when one thinks about it deeply. Here is why:

First, I have learned I do not know what the best outcome is. I absolutely do not. Nor do you. I may think I do, but over the years I have experienced too many instances where my outcome did not work out. That would be the outcome I controlled and forced to go my way. What a fool I was to ever think I knew what was best. And to think I knew better than the Lord? Pompous, preposterous, and even deluded. Like a silly king strutting about with no clothes on.

Please tell me you are not still so deluded. My child, if you are still insisting on having your way, you are missing it badly. If you are still trying to control the outcome, for you, for your business, for your wife or husband, or for your children and their future, you are stumbling around in the dark.

And I can assure you, you will look back and see this clearly one day. Why not let that day be today?

When I abandon the outcome to my loving Heavenly Father, it always turns out to be a far better outcome than I had wanted or envisioned. Surely you have experienced this as well. A far better outcome … an immeasurably better outcome!

Our friend Paul put it this way in his letter to the Family of Followers in Ephesus:

> Now to him who is able to do immeasurably more than all we ask or imagine, according to his power that is at work within us, to him be glory in the church and in Christ Jesus throughout all generations, forever and ever! Amen.

When Saul writes, "… immeasurably more than all we ask or imagine …," he is assuring you Jesus will surprise you with an outcome for which you could not have even imagined to ask of him. That is, if you allow him to lead.

Amen.

First, I have realized I do not know the best outcome. And second, I know he does. I know beyond a shadow of a doubt he does. He knows what is best, and he will do what is best.

I have also learned this truth: I cannot control the outcome. I cannot; you cannot. I never have controlled the outcome, and I never will. If you think you do, you are deluded. And no doubt the people around you are suffering. Because when you are sure you can control the outcome, or that you must, you white-knuckle everything and everyone, maintaining an ever-tightening grip, causing yourself and everyone around you pressure, stress and anxiety.

I want you, dear child, to think deeply about why you won't abandon the outcome to your loving Heavenly Father? What is holding you back from total surrender? What part of you still insists on control, when you have Jesus with you always, and the Holy Spirit indwelling you?

CONTROL

Later, in an interesting turn of events, this same royal official approached me in Capernaum. He said, "John bar-Zebedee, after my encounter with the Master and his healing of my son, I was born again. My whole life started to change. The Holy Spirit filled me, and I started to experience so much love, joy, peace and patience."

His smile then turned to a frown, and he slowly shook his head and said, "But I now have a new position in Herod Antipas' government, and it is very stressful. In my previous role I had much more control. The servants under me did exactly what I said because I had trained them well.

"But now I do not have as much control over the outcome. So I am feeling a lot more stress," he continued. "I thought I had grown out of all that. It frustrates me that I have returned to my old ways."

I looked at him, smiled and said, "My dear new Brother, you never controlled the outcome in your last position. You just thought you did, perhaps because most things went your way. But that was just an illusion."

A few months later he approached me again. He pulled me aside and with a big grin on his face said, "What an idiot I must have seemed to you the last time we spoke. I talked as if I had always been in control. I see now I do not, and I cannot control anything: not my wife, my work, my health, not even my children."

I put my arm around him and smiled. He then said, "And the freedom this clarity has brought me is absolutely wonderful! My stress level is down and I am now so much more relaxed – and everyone around me is too. Thank you for pointing me back to Jesus and his perfect love and his perfect power."

My child, I get really excited talking about abandoning the outcome to Jesus. This is because I have learned over the years that failing to do this becomes the source of most of my stress and anxiety. Regrettably, these thoughts then take over:

"What will I do if this doesn't work out … my way?" "How will I … What if … Who will …?"

And the famous rallying cry of controlling people:

"If I don't, it won't!" – "If it is to be, it is up to me!"

SOUL REST

But there is another way. A quieter, calmer, more relaxed way. It is the way of the Savior:

> "Come to me, all you who are weary and burdened, and I will give you rest. Take my yoke upon you and learn from me, for I am gentle and humble in heart, and you will find rest for your souls. For my yoke is easy and my burden is light."

Notice the following similarity with Yahweh's words through the prophet Jeremiah:

This is what the LORD says:

> "Stand at the crossroads and look;
> ask for the ancient paths,

ask where the good way is, and walk in it,
and you will find rest for your souls."

"Rest for your souls." Soul rest. This is what we are all searching for. Simply put, let Jesus help. Release your grip. Ask him for help. Let him be a part of the process. Involve him. Invite him in, not to try to get the outcome you desire, but invite him into the process – and you will find rest for your soul.

Ask yourself about your soul – is it at rest? Is there a time or a setting when you feel more at peace? What changes in your current lifestyle would it take to capture this soul rest? When the Holy Spirit gives you the clarity to see these answers, I encourage you to act on them!

BUT NOT THE PROCESS

You see, even though we abandon the outcome to Jesus, we do not abandon the process. We have a role to play in the process. A big role. We do our part, and this can include being competitive, proactive, purposeful, even astute and creative. We use our business acumen, our experience, and our judgment to advance the process.

God does not advocate we sit in a closet and pray and expect him to take care of our lives, our children or our businesses. Quite the opposite. Consider these passages:

Saul wrote to the Family in Corinth:

> But by the grace of God I am what I am, and his grace to me was not without effect. No, *I worked harder than all of them*—yet not I, but the grace of God that was with me.

And Peter wrote in his second letter:

> His divine power has given us everything we need for a godly life through our knowledge of him who called us by his own glory and goodness ... For this very reason, *make every effort* to add to your faith ....

Saul and Peter first state that the source of their power comes from God. But they are then quick to point out that we are to "work harder than all of them," and we are to "make every effort ...." And yet, as we do work harder we find a surprising rest for our souls in the midst of our efforts and hard work, because we have involved Jesus in the process. Yes, we have abandoned the outcome to him.

We combine our effort with the presence and power of Jesus, through the Holy Spirit, and together we proceed through the process. Together! We have learned with absolute certainty that we cannot do it on our own. As a matter of fact, a great milestone in my life with Jesus was when I realized I do not even want to do it on my own.

Please do not miss that. When you can grow to this point, when you do not even want to do it on your own, you are going deeper in your walk with the Master. When you truly do not want your desired outcome, unless it is absolutely the desire of Jesus, you are entering the deeper green pastures of the Kingdom.

Saul sums this up nicely in his first letter to the Family in Corinth:

> So whether you eat or drink or whatever you do, do it all for the glory of God.

Remember there is a quieter, calmer, more relaxed way. It is the way of the Savior. I think the following observation captures perfectly the more stressful way:

> A Christian is someone who trusts in the knowledge and the wisdom of God, not in his own abilities. If

> we have a purpose of our own, it destroys the simplicity and the calm, relaxed pace which should be characteristic of the children of God.

Do you have a calm, relaxed pace? Both inside and out?

If we have a purpose, an outcome of our own, then we are not trusting that our Heavenly Father's outcome will be better, and richer than ours. So instead of abandoning the outcome, we have abandoned the calm, relaxed pace that should, and could, be characteristic of a trusting child of God.

> So whether you eat or drink or whatever you do, do it all for the glory of God.

23

DO YOU WANT TO GET WELL?

John 5

We stayed in Cana for the feast the following day, and a couple of days after that. And no, we did not run out of wine! We then returned to Capernaum.

Sometime later, Jesus went up to Jerusalem for one of our Jewish festivals. Now there is in Jerusalem near the Sheep Gate a pool, which in Aramaic is called Bethesda, and which is surrounded by five covered colonnades. This is truly a magnificent site, yet a pitiful one as well. Here a great number of disabled people used to lie—the blind, the lame, the paralyzed.

One who was there had been an invalid for thirty-eight years. When Jesus saw him lying there and learned that he had been in this condition for a long time, he walked over and stood beside him. He then kneeled down and asked him, "Do you want to get well?"

James and I were with Jesus, as he kneeled next to this man. He was pitiful. His legs were shriveled up, as was his soul. He had no hope. He had no future. Thirty-eight years was most of his life. James and I exchanged a look of confusion. Why would

Jesus ask this pitiful man if he wanted to get well? Of course he wanted to get well.

Or did he?

Jesus later explained the reason behind his question. Remember, we have already observed that Jesus did not ask these kinds of questions for his own information. He asked them for our information, and our introspection. He wanted this man to think deeply about what he wanted from Jesus.

It reminded me of when Jesus turned and asked Andrew and me, "What is it you want?" As we said earlier, he was probing us, not for an answer, but for us to answer his question in our minds and in our hearts. Yahweh did the same thing with Adam and Eve in the Garden of Eden. You recall after they ate the fruit Yahweh came walking in the cool of the evening and called out, "Where are you?"

He was not asking where they were hiding physically, he was asking where they were now hiding emotionally and spiritually. It's as if he was saying, not asking, "Do you now see why I commanded you not to eat from the Tree of Good and Evil? Do you see where you are – afraid, naked and hiding in the bushes - now that you have disobeyed me?"

Yahweh does the same thing with Elijah when he is fleeing from Jezebel, after defeating and destroying the four hundred and fifty prophets of Baal on Mt Carmel. Let us pause and revisit this story we find in our first book of Kings, and watch for the "whispering nuance."

> And the word of the LORD came to him: "What are you doing here, Elijah?"
>
> He replied, "I have been very zealous for the LORD God Almighty. The Israelites have rejected your covenant, torn down your altars, and put your prophets to death with the sword. I am the only one left, and now they are trying to kill me too."

> The LORD said, "Go out and stand on the mountain in the presence of the LORD, for the LORD is about to pass by."
>
> Then a great and powerful wind tore the mountains apart and shattered the rocks before the LORD, but the LORD was not in the wind. After the wind there was an earthquake, but the LORD was not in the earthquake. After the earthquake came a fire, but the LORD was not in the fire. And after the fire came a gentle whisper. When Elijah heard it, he pulled his cloak over his face and went out and stood at the mouth of the cave.
>
> Then a voice said to him, "What are you doing here, Elijah?"

Yahweh asks Elijah the same question twice. The LORD is asking Elijah to think deeply about what he is doing. Why is he running for his life? Did Yahweh not just demonstrate his incredible power and his absolute presence by pouring fire from heaven down on Elijah's sacrifice, and defeating the four hundred and fifty prophets of Baal? Given that display of raw cosmic power, why would Elijah now be panicking?

I want you to notice the way Yahweh asked the second time – with a whisper. After the powerful wind tore the mountains apart and shattered the rocks, and after the wind, there was an earthquake, and after the earthquake came a fire, and after the fire came … a gentle whisper.

A gentle whisper. This is the way the Master typically speaks to me now through the Holy Spirit. A gentle whisper. If I am not listening, I will not hear him. If I am too busy, and too distracted, I will not hear him. He will not be heard in the noisy wind of busyness; he is not in the disrupting earthquake of our culture; and he is not in the heat of the fire of incessant activity.

His voice is typically a gentle whisper, meant for those who actually *want* to hear him. For those who are willing to look inside themselves.

Do you want to hear him? Are you willing to look deeply inside?

Perhaps you might want to take a moment and ponder your answer. If Jesus were to ask you, right now, as you read this,

"What are you doing here?"

...what would be your answer?

WHO ARE YOU? WHAT ARE YOU DOING HERE?

There is a story the rabbis tell about this piercing and penetrating introspective question.

One evening a rabbi was returning home, but a deep fog rolled in as the darkness settled around him. At a fork in the road, he took the wrong way, and soon enough he heard a loud, challenging voice calling out, "Who are you? What are you doing here?"

The rabbi realized he had stumbled upon a Roman outpost. He froze for a moment, and the voice came back again, bellowing out the same two questions: "Who are you? What are you doing here?"

The rabbi responded, "What is your daily wage, guard?"

The Roman was taken aback, but then replied, "One denarius, Jew, what is that to you?

The rabbi said, "I will double that if you will come to my home each morning and ask me those same two questions!"

Oh my.

As Jesus is standing over this lame man, he wants him to think deeply about what he wanted. Something we should all make a habit of doing. Was he ready to assume a new life? A life that would require a whole new path for him? He would suddenly be responsible for his day-to-day care and provision. He would now have to take care of himself. He would have to be proactive, no longer lying around and waiting on others to help him.

Was he indeed ready for this? Did he want it? Or ... had he become comfortable being the victim.

VICTIM OR VICTORY?

I have observed over the years that some people like being a victim. Perhaps someone did them wrong somewhere along the way, and yes, they were indeed victimized. But it seems they begin to like being the victim. They like having people feel sorry for them.

Oh, they would never admit this, but it is nevertheless true. Being a victim means they do not have to look inwardly to assess their role or their responsibility in their situation. Perhaps the Samaritan woman at the well had experienced a taste of this. If one is a perpetual victim, then it is always someone else's fault – never one's own. A victim does not have to face any blame, because they are always blaming the other person.

If one is a victim, one never has to change, to grow, to mature. The people I have observed who have become comfortable in the role of victim do not ever seem to grow out of it. They remain the person they have been – a person who is contributing to their own misery.

Being a victim places the burden of being happy and content on someone else. Someone other than the victim must become their provider of happiness and contentment, which is always beyond the victim's reach. And so the cycle continues, because the victim's inability to find happiness and contentment is never their own fault.

They can wallow in a lame, victim position for "thirty-eight years," much like this man at the Bethesda pool.

When Jesus asked the lame man if he wanted to get well, there was a moment, a hesitation, a look between Jesus and this crippled man. There was some kind of communication going on, but not with words. It was deep calling unto deep.

"Sir," the invalid finally replied, "I have no one to help me into the pool when the water is stirred. While I am trying to get in, someone else goes down ahead of me."

Then Jesus said to him, "Get up! Pick up your mat and walk." At once the man was cured; he picked up his mat and walked. I think he was so stunned he just walked off. He did not turn back to Jesus. He did not draw any attention to himself. No one else seemed to notice because there were so many people milling about.

I watched Jesus as he watched this man walk off. He slowly turned to James and me, a slight smile on his face. But he said nothing, and we asked nothing. We just started walking again with him through the crowded street.

But the day on which this took place was a Sabbath, and so the Jewish leaders saw the man carrying his mat and said to the man, "It is the Sabbath; the law forbids you to carry your mat." But he replied, "The man who made me well said to me, 'Pick up your mat and walk.'"

So they asked him, "Who is this fellow who told you to pick it up and walk?" The man who was healed had no idea who it was, for Jesus had slipped away into the crowd.

Later Jesus found him at the temple and said to him, "See, you are well again. Stop sinning or something worse may happen to you." The man went away and told the Jewish leaders that it was Jesus who had made him well.

So, because Jesus was doing these things on the Sabbath, the Jewish leaders began to persecute him. Jesus did not back down, but stated plainly, "My Father is always at his work to this very day, and I too am working." For this reason they tried all the more to kill him; not only was he breaking the Sabbath, but he was even calling God his own Father, making himself equal with God.

This threat would become a constant theme in our lives. The Jewish authorities were in an ongoing state of aggravation, growing stronger over the ensuing months. They were almost panicking over the popularity of Jesus. Who could blame them? Even though he was in no way subverting our Torah, nor was he bringing any type of "new, heretical teaching," he was still a threat to them.

He was a threat to the Sadducees' hold over the temple, and the honor this afforded them, as well as the lucrative money-making temple sacrificial system they exploited. The Sadducees ran the temple. They would exploit the people coming to make sacrifices by charging exorbitant rates for exchanging the pilgrims' coins for temple coins, as well as charging high prices for the purchase of sacrificial animals. It was their power structure and profit model, and they intended to protect it.

The Pharisees were not as worried about their position or status; they were genuinely upset that this man was comparing himself to God. That simply could not stand. They had to stop him. And some sincerely thought Jesus was a heretic, a false prophet.

So the combined forces of the Sadducees and the Pharisees – i.e. the Sanhedrin, our governing body – were determined to expose this upstart rabbi from Galilee, and stop his ministry before it gained any more traction.

But Jesus was only doing what he promised at the beginning of his ministry. Matthew captured this in his gospel account, at the beginning of Jesus' Sermon on the Mount:

> "Do not think that I have come to abolish the Law or the Prophets; I have not come to abolish them but to fulfill them. For truly I tell you, until heaven and earth disappear, not the smallest letter, not the least

stroke of a pen, will by any means disappear from the Law until everything is accomplished."

24

A HARD TEACHING

Now at this point I could spend time telling you about what happened next - Jesus feeding the five thousand, and his walking on water, but you can read about those in the other gospel accounts. Matthew, Mark, and Dr. Luke do a fine job telling those stories. You would do well to read them.

But as I mentioned at the outset, I want to bring you closer to Jesus through his encounters with a select group of individuals. This is my purpose, and I believe it is the Holy Spirit's purpose as well. So I will stick to it, despite the multitude of stories, teachings and miracles. Jesus did many other things as well. If every one of them were written down, I suppose that even the whole world would not have room for the books that would be written.

But before we move on to the next encounter, please let me share with you a conflict that erupted around this time. Jesus was teaching in the synagogue at Capernaum and the Jewish authorities were harassing him. In the midst of their arguing, Jesus stepped back and declared,

> "I am the bread of life. Whoever comes to me will never go hungry, and whoever believes in me will never be thirsty. But as I told you, you have seen me and still you do not believe."

At this the Jews there began to grumble about him because he also said, "I am the bread that came down from heaven." They said, "Is this not Jesus, the son of Joseph, whose father and mother we know? How can he now say, 'I came down from heaven'?"

But Jesus responded,

> "Stop grumbling among yourselves." No one can come to me unless the Father who sent me draws them, and I will raise them up at the last day. No one has seen the Father except the one who is from God; only he has seen the Father. Very truly I tell you, the one who believes has eternal life."

There was a growing murmur among the crowd, but Jesus was undaunted. So he continued, his voice louder and more punctuated:

> "I am the bread of life. Your ancestors ate the manna in the wilderness, yet they died. But here is the bread that comes down from heaven, which anyone may eat and not die. I am the living bread that came down from heaven. Whoever eats this bread will live forever. This bread is my flesh, which I will give for the life of the world."

Then the Jews began to argue sharply among themselves, "How can this man give us his flesh to eat?" They were incredulous, and I have to admit we were amazed, and a bit shocked at the Master's words. What did he mean by all this? James looked at Peter, who shrugged his shoulders and looked back at Jesus. Andrew looked at me, but I was dumbfounded.

Then Jesus drove a dagger into their hearts with his most confusing and startling words they – or we - had ever heard:

> "Very truly I tell you, unless you eat the flesh of the Son of Man and drink his blood, you have no life in you. Whoever eats my flesh and drinks my blood has eternal life, and I will raise them up at the last day. For my flesh is real food and my blood is real drink. Whoever eats my flesh and drinks my blood remains in me, and I in them. Just as the living Father sent me and I live because of the Father, so the one who feeds on me will live because of me. "

Jesus kept his eyes fixed on the Jewish authorities. They were locked in a cold stare. I have to admit I am glad he was not looking at me, because I was struggling to understand the meaning of his words. And I was struggling as to why he would pick this kind of fight with these men. I wondered what my fellow disciples were thinking, but it did not take long to find out.

On hearing it, many of his disciples (not the core group of the Twelve, but those who had been following Jesus for the past several months) said, "This is a hard teaching. Who can accept it?" The crowd was grumbling among themselves, and some were drifting off, trying not to be conspicuous in their departure, but departing, nevertheless.

Aware that they were grumbling about this, Jesus turned and said to them,

> "Does this offend you? Then what if you see the Son of Man ascend to where he was before! The Spirit gives life; the flesh counts for nothing. The words I have spoken to you—they are full of the Spirit and life."

At this time many of his disciples turned back and no longer followed him. Just when I thought things were going so well, and we were gaining disciples, Jesus seemed intent on running them off. We were all deep in our thoughts; I am sure some of us were wondering who among us would also leave. The nervous anxiety was palpable. I do not remember ever feeling so uncomfortable in the presence of the Master.

But uncomfortable we were. Jesus was watching the crowd disperse, and his followers leaving him. I could not tell what he was thinking, but he then turned to us and let his eyes fall on each one of us. The look on his face was challenging. He was not angry, but gone was the loving, compassionate, best-friend look.

He stepped towards us, paused to look each of us in the eye, and said, "You do not want to leave too, do you?"

I have never been so glad for bombastic Simon Peter to shoot off his mouth first. So often his impetuous answers jumped out of his mouth before he thought about it, but on this occasion he captured perfectly the only answer any of us could possibly give:

> "Lord, to whom shall we go? You have the words of eternal life. We have come to believe and to know that you are the Holy One of God."

Yes, and amen!

Yes, by this time we had come to know, know beyond a shadow of a doubt, that this man, this prophet, this rabbi, this builder from Nazareth, was the Holy One of God. His early days may have been spent building with his father Joseph, but for the rest of his life, and now ours, he would be building the foundation for his Kingdom among us.

A Kingdom in which whoever enters will never go hungry, and in which whoever believes in Jesus will never be thirsty. A Kingdom in which the Spirit gives life; the flesh counts for nothing. A Kingdom where whoever drinks the water Jesus gives them will never thirst, but even more so the water he gives them will become in them a spring of water welling up to eternal life.

A Kingdom where the true worshipers will worship the Father in the Spirit and in truth, for they are the kind of worshipers the Father seeks. God is spirit, and his worshipers must worship in the Spirit and in truth.

A Kingdom of the born again.

25

A YOUNG WOMAN IN TROUBLE

John 8

After this, Jesus went around in Galilee. He did not want to go about in Judea because the Jewish leaders there were looking for a way to kill him. It wasn't that he was afraid of them. We knew that. What we did not know at the time, but would understand later, was that Jesus had a plan – his Father's plan – and whether or not he was fully aware of the specific timing, he had an inner sense of what to do and not to do at any given time

He would let his Father's plan play out, in the Father's timing. A valuable lesson for all of us. Peter captured this perfectly in his first letter to the Family of Followers of the Way:

> Humble yourselves, therefore, under God's mighty hand, that he may lift you up in due time.

"In due time." That is the part over which most of us stumble. We did not understand then, but would later see clearly that Jesus was eventually going to force the Jewish authorities' hands at just the right time – the Passover feast. But for now we followed our rabbi around the various towns and synagogues of

Galilee. This suited all of us. Jerusalem did not feel safe, but our beloved Galilee certainly did.

The Pharisees in the Galilee area were not necessarily looking to kill Jesus. Some actually became his followers. Often they would debate Jesus, as they did with each other, over the finer points of the Torah. Pharisees and rabbis are constantly challenging each other over our Holy Scriptures. This is the way of the Jew. We love to debate. We love to discuss.

It may appear we are quarreling with each other, but we are just seeking a better, deeper understanding of our sacred scripture. As I said before, if you have three rabbis gathered together, you will have five opinions!

But when the Jewish Festival of Tabernacles was near, Jesus' brothers said to him, sarcastically I might add, "Leave Galilee and go to Judea, so that your disciples there may see the works you do. No one who wants to become a public figure acts in secret. Since you are doing these things, show yourself to the world."

They were goading him, for even his own brothers did not believe in him. Would you? If you grew up with a big brother, as I did with James, and one day he started telling everyone he was the Son of God, would you not have a hard time accepting that?

His brothers certainly did. But not his mother, Mary. During the years after Jesus' death, when I was taking care of Mary, she would recount stories of Jesus' birth, and all the different times during his childhood that she could see how uniquely gifted he was. She would close her eyes, as if she were transporting herself back to those simpler, safer days, and each time she would finish her stories with, "Now John, I have treasured up all these things and pondered them in my heart these many years."

The Feast of Tabernacles is one of the three festivals that all Jewish men are required to attend. It celebrates the Father's provision during the forty years of the wilderness wandering, as well as the fall harvest of grapes and olives and such. It is a fall festival, and little did we know, but we were just a few months before Jesus' death.

Even though the brothers were trying to goad their big brother, Jesus would not allow them – or anyone for that matter – to force his hand. So he told them,

> "My time is not yet here; for you any time will do. The world cannot hate you, but it hates me because I testify that its works are evil. You go to the festival. I am not going up to this festival, because my time has not yet fully come."

AT THE FESTIVAL

After he had said this, he stayed in Galilee. However, after his brothers had left for the festival, he went also, not publicly, but in secret. Now at the festival the Jewish leaders were watching for Jesus and asking, "Where is he?" Among the crowds there was widespread whispering about him. Some said, "He is a good man." Others replied, "No, he deceives the people." But no one would say anything publicly about him for fear of the leaders – the Sanhedrin.

The Pharisees heard the crowd whispering such things about him. So the chief priests and the Pharisees sent temple guards to arrest him. But the people were so impressed, and quite frankly so energized over Jesus, the guards were flummoxed as to what to do. I have to admit it was somewhat comical, watching them argue and debate among themselves about approaching Jesus. These rough, tough guards just could not seem to bring themselves to arrest him. It was almost as if he had cast a spell over them … a power they could not discern. Or more likely, the Father put in their hearts that this was not a man to be reckoned with. At least not for now.

Finally, the temple guards went back to the chief priests and the Pharisees, who were extremely aggravated at seeing them returning without Jesus. In a gruff tone they asked them, "Why didn't you bring him in?"

Nicodemus told us what happened next, and as he told us the story, he could not help but laugh. The guards were standing before the Sanhedrin, clearly uncomfortable, fidgeting and looking down. Finally, one of them said in an exasperated tone, raising his arms in the air, palms up.

"No one ever spoke the way this man does," the guard replied. Now this really angered these august men, so they snorted out, "You mean he has deceived you also? Have any of the rulers or the Pharisees believed in him? No! But this mob that knows nothing of the law—there is a curse on them." Their faces were red and contorted as they shouted at the guards.

In the midst of all of this Nicodemus asked, "Does our law condemn a man without first hearing him to find out what he has been doing?" He was sincere in his question, but he told us he was also enjoying the moment, challenging his fellow Sanhedrin.

They replied, "Are you from Galilee, too? Look into it, and you will find that a prophet does not come out of Galilee."

On the surface that sounds like a ridiculous statement, as several notable prophets had come from Galilee. But I assume they meant The Prophet, the one Moses prophesied in Deuteronomy:

> The LORD said to me: "What they say is good. I will raise up for them a prophet like you from among their fellow Israelites, and I will put my words in his mouth. He will tell them everything I command him."

STONE HER!

During the feast we were spending our nights on the Mount of Olives. Martha and Mary and Lazarus lived nearby in Bethany, with their father Simon the Leper. They would often have us over for meals. Jesus loved them deeply. He and Lazarus seemed to have connected in a deep way. They would laugh together about things to which we were not privy. It bothered Simon Peter a bit, this deep relationship Jesus had apart from us, but we could see Lazarus brought great joy to Jesus.

At dawn the next day Jesus appeared again in the temple courts, where all the people gathered around him, and he sat down to teach them. The crowds were amazed at his teaching, because he taught as one who had authority, and not as their teachers of the law. We could hear them whisper among themselves, "How did this man get such learning without having been taught?" Many in the crowd believed in him. They said, "When the Messiah comes, will he perform more signs than this man?"

Notice that yet again it is the way Jesus taught with authority that made such an impression on the people. The Master taught as if he owned the place – the temple - which of course he did. Jesus did not quote other rabbis or sources. He was the Source. He was the Rabbi. I remember listening to Jesus as he began his Sermon on the Mount as he said, "You have heard that it was said, but I say to you…."

"I say." Not, "Others say." Not, even as Moses and the prophets would often say, "The LORD says." Jesus said, emphatically, "I say" ("because I do indeed own the place.")

We were all with Jesus that morning as he was teaching the crowd around him, near Solomon's Porch. The sun was rising to the middle of the sky, and the day was warming. There was a lovely breeze (Was it the Holy Spirit?). Jesus' words and the warm sun left me completely relaxed. Everyone was engrossed in Jesus' words when suddenly there was a commotion. The crowd parted and an angry group of Pharisees came storming up to Jesus. Their guards dragged a young woman along with them. She was bedraggled and barely clothed. One look at her terrified face and I knew she was in deep trouble.

The Jewish authorities had caught this woman in adultery. They made her stand before the group, and glaring at Jesus, demanded of him, "Teacher, this woman was caught in the act of adultery. In the Law, Moses commanded us to stone such women. Now what do you say?" They were using this question as a trap, in order to have a basis for accusing him.

You see, the Romans did not allow us to punish anyone with death. They reserved that right for themselves. It happened from time to time, as with Stephen's stoning, but it was a rare occurrence. This trap was set up to give Jesus no way out. If he said, "Yes, she should be stoned as the Torah commands," these men would rush over to Pilate and tell him Jesus was subverting Roman law.

That would be a death sentence for Jesus. And possibly for us, as well. But if he said, "No, she should not be stoned," they would use this to discredit him among the Jews. They would tell everyone, "This man does not respect and uphold our Torah!" That would be a practical death sentence to his authoritative standing with the people.

Jesus saw right through their machinations. Even I could see the trap; it was that obvious. Yet I was at a loss as to how Jesus could respond. I was holding my breath, not knowing what to expect next. I could hear the crowd murmuring behind me: "What is he going to do?" They have the Teacher in a trap."

The tension was palpable. I felt like time stood still. What would Jesus do? Well, he did something no one could have predicted. He did something no one I know of has ever done in the face of this kind of hostility.

He bent down.

JESUS KNEELED DOWN

Yes, he kneeled. And it was as if the world came to a halt. The breeze stopped. It seemed as though all the chatter one hears all around the temple went mute. If I had had the eyes of the Master I might have even seen angels stopping to watch.

He kneeled down and started to write in the sand with his finger. This startled the men for a moment, as it did us. They stared at him, lost as to what he was doing. But then they gathered themselves and kept on questioning him, their tone still angry and accusing. After a couple of moments, the Master straightened up and said to them, "Let any one of you who is without sin be the first to throw a stone at her." Again, he stooped down and wrote in the sand.

We were all wondering what would happen next. I could hear some of the crowd that had been listening to Jesus teaching whispering among themselves. "What is he doing? Is he that afraid of the authorities?" Another said, "He doesn't look at all afraid. But they suddenly look terrified!"

The woman was on her knees, her face downcast and staring at the ground, tears were falling, and sweat was dripping from her brow. The sun was beating down on us, and the glare partly blinded me. The Pharisees and teachers of the law stood still, a look of confusion on their faces. As the seconds ticked by their intense rage began to fade.

They were in the wrong and they knew it. They had not even brought the man who was caught with this woman. It was a setup and suddenly they were exposed for the hypocrites they were. They obviously had not been expecting Jesus to respond the way he did.

In retrospect, as they stood there, totally flummoxed, Jesus' response must have reminded these experts in the scriptures of two passages from our Hebrew Scriptures.

The first is from Deuteronomy:

> On the testimony of two or three witnesses a person is to be put to death, but no one is to be put to death on the testimony of only one witness. The hands of

> the witnesses must be the first in putting that person to death, and then the hands of all the people.

The second is from our prophet Jeremiah. And this is the one that I believe stung them the most:

> Lord, you are the hope of Israel; all who forsake
> you will be put to shame.
> Those who turn away from you will be written in
> the dust because they have forsaken the Lord, the
> spring of living water.

They knew Jesus was acting out this passage from Jeremiah. He was acting out a living Remez. A Remez is a technique the rabbis often use when teaching. They recite a portion of scripture, knowing their Jewish audience will be familiar with the passage, and so immediately their listeners will think of the entire passage and the implications of the teaching in that passage.

These men knew Jesus was indicating, by writing in the sand that, "you will be written in the dust because you have forsaken the Lord, the spring of living water." Without looking at each other, those who heard began to go away one at a time, the older ones first, until only Jesus was left, with the woman still standing there.

They all walked away. We were stunned. I kept my eyes on Jesus, but I could sense and hear the murmurs around me. Some of those who had been listening to Jesus teach just a few moments before were saying, "Did you just see what I saw? The Jewish authorities all walked away." Another quickly added, "Slinked away is more like it."

Others said, "Did you see the teacher kneel down? I was expecting anything but that. I thought he might challenge the leaders. I was transfixed by what I was watching, but I never expected him to kneel down and write in the dust!"

Still others were saying, "He not only teaches with a new authority, but he also acts with a new authority!"

I watched Jesus as he leaned over and gently took the woman by the chin and carefully lifted her face up. He straightened himself up, looked around, and asked her, "Woman, where are they? Has no one condemned you?"

"No one, sir," she said, her face looking down, tears streaming, unable to look Jesus in the eye.

"Then neither do I condemn you," Jesus said, with a kind smile. "Go now and leave your life of sin. I can see into your heart, and I know you are hurting, and I know you do not want to live this way. I can fill those holes in your heart, if only you will let me."

There was a moment, a hesitation, a look between Jesus and this woman. They held each other's gaze. I saw it and felt a stirring in my soul. There was some kind of communication going on, but not with words. It was deep calling unto deep.

She smiled weakly, nodded almost imperceptibly, and slowly walked away, glancing back at the man who had just saved her life. Later, she would join us and become one of the many women who followed Jesus. Each of them because, in one way or another, he had healed and filled the holes in their hearts.

Of course, that is what he does for all of us who follow him. He heals our hearts by filling all the holes we have in our hearts.

NO CONDEMNATION

"Then neither do I condemn you."

Saul would later write in his letters to the Family of Followers in Rome,

> Therefore, there is now no condemnation for those who are in Christ Jesus, because through Christ Jesus the law of the Spirit who gives life has set you free from the law of sin and death.

Please let this sink in. This is a powerful teaching for all of us. In the Kingdom of the Father, there is no condemnation, only conviction. We just saw Jesus convict, but not condemn this young woman, by telling her, "Go now and leave your life of sin." He is saying, "I do not condemn you, you are not a failure, but stop living this way. Adultery is no life for a precious young daughter of the Father like you."

Condemnation comes from Satan – the Accuser. When you hear a voice of condemnation and accusation in your head it is never from the Father. It is always from the Accuser. Please, trust me on this. Satan's condemning voice whispers, "What a failure you are! You will never do any better. If only others could see the real you. You should keep your distance from God. Let him cool off a bit. He is so disappointed in you."

Lies. All lies. Instead of keeping your distance, run to your Heavenly Father. Fall at his knees and confess your sins. What you will hear in return will be his loving words of assurance and compassion. Just as in Dr. Luke's gospel, and the wayward son returning home to his father, your Heavenly Father will run to you, not wait on you to grovel for acceptance. I remember sitting with big brother James as Jesus told the story about the love and gracious forgiveness of the Father:

> "When he came to his senses, he said, 'How many of my father's hired servants have food to spare, and here I am starving to death! I will set out and go back to my father and say to him: Father, I have sinned against heaven and against you. I am no longer worthy to be called your son; make me like one of your hired servants.' So he got up and went to his father.
>
> "But while he was still a long way off, his father saw him and was filled with compassion for him; he ran to his son, threw his arms around him and kissed him.

> "The son said to him, 'Father, I have sinned against heaven and against you. I am no longer worthy to be called your son.'
>
> "But the father said to his servants, 'Quick! Bring the best robe and put it on him. Put a ring on his finger and sandals on his feet. Bring the fattened calf and kill it. Let's have a feast and celebrate. For this son of mine was dead and is alive again; he was lost and is found.'" So they began to celebrate.

This is compassion with conviction, but no condemnation. There is no condemnation after we are born again; we are cleansed from all sin. We are holy and blameless in the Father's eyes, without sin and free from accusation.

Free from accusation! Free from the accuser!

The convicting voice of your loving Heavenly Father says, "I know you have sinned. But my Son has already paid the price for your sin. I want you to pick yourself up and look to the future, not your past. Your sins are removed from you as far as the east is from the west. You can live better, and you and I know it. I want a better life for you. So stop living this way."

26

AMAZING GRACE

May I reflect a little more on what just happened? How the Master masterfully diffused what could have been a disaster for both himself and this young woman?

As these dogmatic Pharisees came storming over with this poor young woman caught in adultery, I could hear them saying, even if only in their hearts, "Why shouldn't we stone her? She is not perfect, as we are. She showed human weakness; something we never do. She must be condemned!"

Jesus is facing a setting seething with condemnation, judgment and human weakness, yet he responds with grace and compassion. Grace and compassion are Jesus' way of strength, not power and aggression. Only weak men rely on power and aggression.

True strength is meek strength. Meek strength is power under control.

If it had been me, I would have stepped toward the Pharisees with my chest out, ready to control the situation and react with my strength. A Son of Thunder! (I know Simon Peter would have.)

But Jesus did not do this, did he? He knelt down. Instead of powering up, he powered down. And in so doing he sucked all the negative, hostile energy out of the air. The Pharisees were expecting a fight; they got finesse. They were seeking confrontation, instead they received calm. They were looking for an overreaction, instead they got a measured response.

Jesus never reacts in fear; he always responds in faith.

Jesus diffused the strain and stress of the situation, and ultimately the Pharisees retreated. Jesus' guiding principle came from Zechariah's words,

> "Not by might nor by power, but by my Spirit," says the Lord Almighty.

POWER DOWN

Jesus taught and modeled this in so many ways over the time we were together. Here is just a sampling of his words about powering down versus powering up, that are so dear to my heart:

> "Blessed are the meek, for they will inherit the earth. Blessed are the merciful, for they will be shown mercy. Blessed are the peacemakers, for they will be called children of God."
>
> "You have heard that it was said, 'Eye for eye, and tooth for tooth.' But I tell you, do not resist an evil person. If anyone slaps you on the right cheek, turn to them the other cheek also."
>
> "And if anyone wants to sue you and take your shirt, hand over your coat as well."
>
> "If anyone forces you to go one mile, go with them two miles. Give to the one who asks you, and do not turn away from the one who wants to borrow from you."

Power down, not power up. That is amazing grace.

Grace creates and engenders relationships. When I feel that someone "takes me as I am," extending grace to my fragile, flawed self, the intimacy of friendship deepens. Very few of us do this well. We judge. We try to fix. And often, in our inner hearts, we condemn.

We do this throughout our daily interactions, but most damagingly we do this with our families. Men especially do this by powering up. But not just men. (Ladies, check yourselves, too.) Many times I have had to confront a highly successful man and say, "Listen to me. Stop with the powering up. What may work at work, does not work at home."

Powering up, raising our voices, sticking out our chests, intimidating others – these are the techniques we think are necessary, and, yes, they may appear to work at work. But what works at work does not work at home with your family, with your friends, or with your Self. And certainly not with Jesus.

Powering up is the world's way, not Jesus' way.

> "There is now no condemnation for those who are in Christ Jesus."

Jesus is reaching out to you today and saying "Yes, I will take you as you are. I will not try to force a fix on you all at once, but I will start to heal you. I will even transform you, that is, if you will get off your throne of Self and let me. I will never condemn you, but through the Holy Spirit I will convict you of those areas of your life holding you back from my 'Life to the Full.'"

When we are living in the Kingdom – not just living in religion - Jesus convicts, but never condemns. As the Holy Spirit moved Paul to write in his first letter to the Corinthians:

> I am saying this for your own good, not to restrict you, but that you may live in a right way in undivided devotion to the Lord.

I learned this during my time with the Master, and I want you to see Jesus as we saw him: "full of grace and truth." This is why I am focusing this story on his encounters with others. By presenting you with several living parables, highlighting Jesus' delicate and grace-full balance of grace and truth, I hope to show you the true heart of Jesus. This is why this story of this woman caught in adultery is one of my favorites.

Jesus is presented with this poor woman's human weakness, and at the same time he is confronted with the condemnation of these seemingly powerful men. But Jesus diffuses their power, and their condemnation. He powers down, instead of powering up. He draws the attention away from the woman and onto himself.

As I have reflected on this volatile drama and how it unfolded, I see this as an act of grace in action – a living parable. When was the last time you, when confronted with anger and condemnation, knelt down?

I tend to meet power with power. You judge me, I'll judge you. You attack me, I'll counterattack you. If you point out my weaknesses, I go into automatic vindication mode, ready to defend myself. How about you? Looking back over the years, I can see what Jesus was trying to show us here: this powering up approach does not work. It does not endear relationship; it injures relationship.

Jesus absorbs all the negative energy of these angry men, and then he turns the tables on them when he responds with, "If any one of you is without sin, let him be the first to throw a stone at her." Notice Jesus did not react, he responded. And then he knelt back down again.

They did not see that coming. They were expecting a confrontation. Jesus gave them conviction. They wanted to condemn Jesus. He instead convicted them. So they left. Their power drained. Their negative energy and condemnation towards the woman were absorbed by Jesus. He took the blame away from her and onto himself.

He modeled our fifteenth proverb,

> A gentle answer turns away wrath,
> but a harsh word stirs up anger.

He will do the same for you. I hope you know this. He lavished grace on this terrified woman, but also with the truth she needed to hear.

This is the way of the Master.

27

BORN BLIND

John 9

I want to share with you Jesus' next healing encounter, not so much because of his interaction with this man who was born blind, but because of the almost comical back and forth that ensued between this now-seeing blind man, and the still-cannot-see blind Sanhedrin. We all need a little levity, especially in light of the events that would soon follow.

After the young girl who had been caught in adultery walked away, Jesus left the temple and walked through the narrow streets of Jerusalem. You recall we were in Jerusalem for the Feast of Tabernacles, which is in the fall, after the last harvest of olives and grapes and such. The air was cooling a bit and the sun was shining brilliantly in the Judean sky. It was a perfect fall day and Jesus was clearly enjoying his time in his Father's beloved city.

As he went along, he saw a man blind from birth. Jesus paused, so we asked him, "Rabbi, who sinned, this man or his parents, that he was born blind?"

In our culture blindness, or leprosy, or for that matter most any misfortune that might befall someone, even and especially poverty, is due to their sin. Or their parents' sin. In our culture, one is either blessed by Yahweh, and therefore financially and physically well off, or one is in disfavor with Yahweh, and therefore sick, or poor, or both.

This thought process derives from Yahweh's words in our book of Exodus, as he is giving us the commandment about no idols:

> You shall not bow down to them or worship them; for I, the LORD your God, am a jealous God, punishing the children for the sin of the parents to the third and fourth generation of those who hate me, but showing love to a thousand generations of those who love me and keep my commandments.

Now first, please notice the "1000 to 3" ratio of blessings to punishment. The Father's promises of 1000 generations blessed, compared to 3 generations punished, is overwhelming in his grace, mercy and compassion. But this "punishment" is more a fact of life, than any punishing action by God. When one considers that in our culture families often live together in the father's compound, the bet 'ab, for several generations, naturally a father's sin is going to negatively affect the children, in effect "punishing" them, because they all live together. The consequences of his sin become their punishment.

But a more helpful passage to consider is found in our fifth and final Torah book, Deuteronomy:

> Parents are not to be put to death for their children, nor children put to death for their parents; each will die for their own sin.

And the prophet Ezekiel expounds on this as well:

> But suppose this son has a son who sees all the sins his father commits, and though he sees them, he does not do such things.
>
> He will not die for his father's sin; he will surely live.
>
> The child will not share the guilt of the parent, nor will the parent share the guilt of the child. The righteousness of the righteous will be credited to them, and the wickedness of the wicked will be charged against them.

Jesus pondered the blind man for a moment, and then turned to us and said, "Neither this man nor his parents sinned, but this happened so that the works of God might be displayed in him. As long as it is day, we must do the works of him who sent me. Night is coming, when no one can work. While I am in the world, I am the light of the world."

After saying this, he spit on the ground, made some mud with the saliva, and put it on the man's eyes. "Go," he told him, "wash in the Pool of Siloam" (Siloam means "Sent"). So the man went and washed, and came home seeing.

This man, his name was Jacob, later told us what happened next.

As he returned to his neighborhood, his neighbors and those who had formerly seen him blind and begging, approached him and gathered around him. They were startled by the sight of Jacob's sight. They looked at each other and asked, "Isn't this the same man who used to sit and beg?" Some claimed that he was. Others said, "No, he only looks like him." But he himself insisted, "I am the man."

"How then were your eyes opened?" they asked him incredulously. He replied, "The man they call Jesus made some mud and put it on my eyes. He told me to go to Siloam and wash. So I went and washed, and then I could see."

"Where is this man?" they asked him. "I don't know," he said.

Don't you just love Jacob's blunt forthrightness? He was not a man to mince words, as we will soon see.

His neighbors were troubled by this shocking turn of events, so they brought Jacob to the Pharisees for them to see this man who had been blind, but could now see. Now the day on which Jesus had made the mud and opened the man's eyes was a Sabbath. As you may know, the Pharisees considered themselves guardians of the commandments in our Torah, and anything that even came close to violating the commandment to keep the Sabbath holy was a flashpoint for them. But Jesus would often call them out on their legalistic approach to matters such as these.

It was not that their hearts were evil, necessarily, at least certainly not all of the Pharisees. After the first destruction of the temple by the Babylonians, the study of the Torah became of utmost importance to these men, because there was no temple at which to sacrifice and worship. Studying the Holy Scriptures then became their form of worship, and these Pharisees took it very seriously.

Of course we all should, and I want you to know that Jesus would tell you that your scripture study is every bit as much a part of your worship as singing or praying.

The Pharisees were so focused on not violating any of the commandments, they built a hedge around them to be certain they did not even get close to violating a commandment. Therefore they added many 'oral laws' to restrict behavior beyond anything called for by Yahweh. They thought they were protecting Yahweh, but in effect, they were hindering his purposes.

FREEDOM

Yahweh gave us the Torah as teachings to help us live the life that is truly life. The commandments were first and foremost guides to his way to live, so that we might thrive and flourish with him. These commandments were given to us in marriage covenant language. They were not intended to be wooden and restrictive. They were meant to be freeing! Freedom from the strongholds that would inhibit the Father's best life, and freedom to live freely.

As the Spirit prompted brother Saul to write in his letter to the Galatians,

> It is for freedom that God has set you free. Stand firm then and do not allow yourselves to be burdened again by a yoke of slavery.

Jesus also told us,

> "If you hold to my teaching, you are really my disciples. Then you will know the truth, and the truth will set you free."

Yes, freedom *from* and freedom *to*. Freedom from the old burdens of rule-keeping and performance, trying to please God and to be good enough to get into heaven. And freedom to live the life that is truly life, with undivided devotion to the Lord.

But the Pharisees did not like the idea of too much freedom, because in their minds it would lead to sin and licentiousness. Particularly when it came to keeping the Sabbath holy. Therefore the Pharisees were blind to the obvious miracle of the blind man's sight, and focused instead on the method – and the Sabbath day.

So they asked him how he had received his sight. "He put mud on my eyes," the man replied, "and I washed, and now I see."

Some of the Pharisees said, "This man is not from God, for he does not keep the Sabbath." But others asked, "How can a sinner perform such signs?" So they were divided. Then they turned again to the blind man, "What have you to say about him? It was your eyes he opened."

TRASH-TALKING

Jacob later told us that he was growing tired of these pious, but pompous men's deliberations and debates, so he decided to rustle their feathers a bit. He replied, "He is a prophet."

But the men were offended by his statement and refused to even consider that he had been blind and received his sight, so they sent for the man's parents. They directed their frustration at his poor parents and demanded, "Is this your son? Is this the one you say was born blind? How is it that now he can see?"

Jacob's parents were terrified, and did not know what to say, so they looked down at the floor and said, meekly, "We know he is our son, and we know he was born blind." They then looked up and the father raised his hands and stammered, "But how he can now see, or who opened his eyes, we don't know. Ask him. He is of age; he will speak for himself."

His parents said this because they were afraid of the Jewish leaders, who already had decided that anyone who acknowledged that Jesus was the Messiah would be put out of the synagogue. And no one wanted to be put out of the synagogue. The synagogue was much more than a "church;" it was the center of social and community activity, as well as for studying and learning the Torah. That was why his parents said, "He is of age; ask him."

By this time the Pharisees were totally agitated by this growing scandal, so a second time they summoned the man who had been blind. "Give glory to God by telling the truth," they said. Then their leader looked directly at Jacob, pointed his finger and said, "We know this man who healed you is a sinner."

By this point Jacob's confidence was growing, as well as his spiritual insight, so he replied, in what has to be one of the all-time most succinct and powerful statements:

"Whether he is a sinner or not, I don't know. One thing I do know. I was blind but now I see!"

"I was blind but now I see."

This "I was blind" certainly describes me before Jesus, and I am equally certain it describes you. As a matter of fact, if I encounter someone who does not yet understand this idea of their own blindness, or cannot make the same declaration, "I was blind but now I see," I can be fairly certain that person is not saved. They do not yet have the Holy Spirit. Therefore, the eyes of their heart have not been opened, nor enlightened.

"I was blind but now I see." I have treasured this declaration all these years.

But these men were not to be put off, so they continued to harass Jacob. Then they asked him, "What did he do to you? How did he open your eyes?"

Jacob told us he was beginning to enjoy himself, and he was amused by the frustration of the authorities, so he answered with an obvious tone of sarcasm. "I have told you already and you did not listen. Why do you want to hear it again? Do you want to become his disciples too?"

Well, this infuriated the men, so with their eyes bulging and their faces red, they hurled insults at him and said, "You are this fellow's disciple! We are disciples of Moses! We know that God spoke to Moses, but as for this fellow, we don't even know where he comes from."

Jacob answered, "Now that is remarkable! You don't know where he comes from, yet he opened my eyes. We know that God does not listen to sinners. He listens to the godly person who does his will. Nobody has ever heard of opening the eyes of a man born blind. If this man were not from God, he could do nothing."

To this they replied, "You were steeped in sin at birth; how dare you lecture us!" And they threw him out.

I WANT TO SEE!

Jesus heard that they had thrown him out, and so he went and found him. He asked him, "Do you believe in the Son of Man?"

Jacob said, "Point him out to me, sir, so that I can believe in him." Jesus replied, "You're looking right at him. Don't you recognize my voice?"

"Master, I believe," Jacob said, and fell to his knees and worshiped him.

Jesus then turned to us and said, "I came into the world to bring everything into the clear light of day, making all the distinctions clear, so that those who have never seen with the spiritual eyes of their hearts will see, and those who have made a great pretense of seeing will be exposed as blind."

Some Pharisees overheard him and said, "Does that mean you're calling us blind?"

Jesus looked them straight in the eye and said, "If you were really blind, you would not be guilty of sin. In a sense you would be blameless. But since you claim to see everything so well, you're accountable for every fault and failure, and your guilt remains. So yes, you are indeed blind – spiritually blinded by your pride."

You see, we are all born blind. The only question is, can we now say with honesty, "But now I see?" One of the Lord's prophets put it this way: "If all you can see is what you can see, then you are not seeing all there is to see."

Again, Saul, prompted by the Holy Spirit, stated this so eloquently in his letter to the Family of Followers in Ephesus,

> I pray that the eyes of your heart may be enlightened in order that you may know the hope to which he has called you, the riches of his glorious inheritance in his holy people, and his incomparably great power for us who believe.

Now, my friend, that is a prayer you can pray for me anytime. In my own prayers I often declare to my Heavenly Father, "I want to see!" Blind Bartimaeus also declared this as we approached Jericho on our final walk to Jerusalem, as Passover was approaching:

> As Jesus and we disciples, together with a large crowd, were leaving the city, a blind man, Bartimaeus (which means "son of Timaeus"), was sitting by the roadside begging. When he heard that it was Jesus of Nazareth, he began to shout, "Jesus, Son of David, have mercy on me!"
>
> Many rebuked him and told him to be quiet, but he shouted all the more, "Son of David, have mercy on me!"
>
> Jesus took hold of Bartimaeus' hand and asked him, "What do you want me to do for you?" (There is that question again.)
>
> Bartimaeus looked up at the sound of Jesus' voice and said, "Rabbi, I want to see."

ALWAYS ALREADY

"Rabbi, I want to see." As I said, this is often my prayer when I am talking with the Father. I hope it will be yours. I want to see with the eyes of Jesus. I want to have the clarity of spiritual eyesight. I want to see beyond the surface. I want to see the real world all around me – the spiritual world. Just as Elisha, in our book of 2 Kings, prayed for his servant when he had panicked at the sight of soldiers from Aram surrounding them,

> "Don't be afraid," the prophet answered. "Those who are with us are more than those who are with them."
>
> And Elisha prayed, "Open his eyes, LORD, so that he may see." Then the LORD opened the servant's eyes, and he looked and saw the hills full of horses and chariots of fire all around Elisha.

Notice Elisha did not pray for the LORD to send angels and horses and chariots of fire. He prayed his servant would see what and who *is already there*. Already and always there – surrounding you and surrounding me.

Always. Already.

This is my prayer. "Open my eyes, LORD, so that I may see, who is always and already surrounding me, in this God-saturated world."

Recall that Jesus told Nicodemus:

> "No one can see the kingdom of God unless they are born again."

I want the eyes of my heart enlightened so I may see what is already all around me. I want to see the Kingdom of God - in all its glory – all around me, day in and day out. Now. The reality of a God-Saturated world. Solomon asked for discernment; I ask for spiritual sight.

Do you see why this miracle was so unique? And why the Jewish authorities were so stiff-necked about it? This was not a healing; Jesus did not heal a disease that had caused Jacob's blindness. He was born blind. No, this was not a healing; it was a new creation! This is why I call this his fourth sign. It pointed to something much larger than a healing miracle. If Jesus could create sight, what else could he do? This rattled the Jewish authorities badly and left them stumbling in their own blindness.

28

RECOVERING RHYTHM

This episode of healing the blind man was one of several healings Jesus performed on the Sabbath. This put him in direct conflict with the Pharisees, who considered themselves guardians of the commandments in our Torah. As I said, anything that even came close to violating the commandment to keep the Sabbath holy was a flashpoint for them.

As the Kingdom was opened to more and more Gentiles, keeping the Sabbath holy and set apart became an issue of contention. Were the Gentiles required to keep the Sabbath? For that matter were Jewish followers of Jesus required to continue to keep the Sabbath holy, since we have been freed from the requirements of the Law?

Allow me to take a moment to address this, since many of you are Gentle followers of the Master. Let us first do away with the idea of rules and requirements, and let us think instead in terms of what is good for us. Remember, when you read "The Law," it is actually "the Torah," which is not about rules and regulations; it is the Father's teachings, and his path to his life to the full.

Remember the Spirit's words through Saul,

> "I am saying this for your own good, not to restrict you, but that you may live in a right way in undivided devotion to the Lord."

Perhaps a conversation we had with Saul on one of his visits to Jerusalem will be helpful. Because Saul was so brilliant and so insightful, he had many questions about things such as how the Torah might apply to the Gentiles. He had only been born again about three or four years when he first came to Jerusalem to see us, but with his keen intellect, and his Hebrew and Greek education and background, he could foresee many questions and challenges about which we had yet to think.

As we sat down for a meal together during Saul's first trip to Jerusalem, I reminded my two friends of Jesus' miracle with this man born blind:

> After saying this, he spit on the ground, made some mud with the saliva, and put it on the man's eyes. "Go," he told him, "wash in the Pool of Siloam" (this word means "Sent"). So the man went and washed, and came home seeing.

"Brother Simon, I said, "you remember that day and exactly how it unfolded, right?" Peter nodded. "Well, have you thought about why the Master spit in the mud?" Peter looked at me and then to Saul, and said, "You know, I have pondered that many times. It did not make sense to me. Why would he do that when we witnessed him heal people far away. Surely he did not need to use the spit and mud?"

Saul looked at me and said, "I may know where you are going with this, John. Are you thinking about the Pharisees' prohibition against spitting on the ground on the Sabbath?" He started to grin and motioned for me to continue.

"Well, men," I responded, "as we know the Rabbis prohibited plowing on the Sabbath, but took it a step further and said spitting in the ground was prohibited because the spit might make a dent in the ground, or move the dirt around, and thus constitute plowing."

Peter rolled his eyes and said, "Took it a step further? That always seemed to be a leap, not a step!"

Saul stood up and said, "Now brother John, you are not suggesting the Master spit in the ground when he healed this blind man to mock the Rabbis, and exacerbate them further, are you?" Saul was grinning now.

"Far be it from me to imply anything untoward with Jesus, my friends," I said, as we were all smiling now, "but knowing his mischievous side, he may have decided to poke them a little bit, and at the same time expose how silly their spitting law was."

We all three got a nice chuckle over the thought.

After a moment, Saul became contemplative, and said, "Simon and John, I know we all observe the Sabbath, but does this commandment apply to the Gentiles? As you know, the Greeks and Romans have a dim view of our Sabbath. To them it is an excuse for laziness. They have no perspective for a day of rest. They work seven days a week."

I nodded in understanding and said, "There are so many things to say about keeping the Sabbath. But let me just make a few observations I think will help you in your discussions with Gentiles."

Saul nodded and motioned for me to continue.

"As you know the fourth commandment to keep the Sabbath is repeated numerous times throughout our Scriptures." Saul nodded in agreement, motioning me to go on. "I say this to say, anything that is important *to* the Father must be important *for* us. We all need a break from the daily and weekly grind, don't we? We need a more relaxed, balanced rhythm to our week, and the Sabbath is God's gift to us for this purpose."

Saul interrupted me and said, "But any time I bring the Sabbath up to the Gentiles, they respond as if I am placing a burden on them. They say, 'What are you talking about? Not doing anything - not anything at all on a particular day? Why, that is too restrictive.'"

"And they will often say something like, 'And that commandment is from your Hebrew scriptures. Did not your Jesus do away with those old requirements? And don't you yourself preach freedom from things such as circumcision? I do not see how keeping the Sabbath is any different.'"

"Saul," I replied, "I would encourage the Gentiles to view this day as a gift from God, not a garret tightening around their throats. It is a gift of rest and reflection, which I can assure you everyone needs."

Saul interrupted me, clearly frustrated, and said, "But they always want specifics on what they can do and what they cannot do on the Sabbath. And I can assure you, "Not working" is not the answer they are looking for. I need to understand better what the Father means by not working, especially when it comes to this Greco-Roman culture in which I live."

TO – FROM

I thought for a moment and then said, "Perhaps if we break down the fourth commandment into two words it will make it easier for them to understand how to receive this gift from God: To and From."

"To and From," Saul frowned. "What does that mean?

I said, "Let's recite the commandment together, and I'll show you what I mean."

So we did, each knowing it by heart, being good Jewish boys.

> "Remember the Sabbath day by keeping it holy. Six days you shall labor and do all your work, but the seventh day is a Sabbath to the LORD your God."

I motioned for Saul to stop. I said, "Brother, do you see here the seventh day is a Sabbath … *to* … the LORD?"

Saul pondered this for a minute and then his eyes lit up. "Yes, I see that. And as the commandment continues God talks about resting *from* our work. I see what you mean by 'To and From,' but explain how this applies to understanding the do's and don'ts for the Sabbath rest."

Peter then spoke up. "Here is what I have found, Saul. Remember, I am a get-it-done, typical male, and I used to be frustrated with the Sabbath day of rest. I was bored out of my mind. It felt so restrictive. I did not know back then just how much my body and my soul needed rest, reflection, and re-energizing. And even worse, my pride was too big to admit that, and my selfishness was too great to give up what I wanted to do.

"But as the Spirit has given me more clarity," he continued, "I see now it is not about a list of dos and don'ts. I now view my possible activities on the Sabbath with this perspective: Will this activity bring me *closer to* the Lord, or move me *away from* him?"

"Bring me closer to or take me farther from," Saul mused. "Okay, there is the "to and from" again. Can you give me an example, Simon?"

Peter said, "Yes, I can. I have found that taking a walk with Ruth in the afternoon of the Sabbath to be very calming and peaceful. We walk in the countryside where it is quiet. It feeds my soul."

Saul interrupted and said, "But what about the commandant not to walk over a Sabbath day's walk? Are you ignoring that commandment?"

"Well, first of all, that is not a commandment. It is an oral interpretation from the rabbis seeking to define what the Father meant by work." Simon Peter said. "You know that as well as I. And Jesus had a way of cutting through those types of oral interpretations by saying, "You have heard that it is said, but I tell you…."

Saul again interrupted and said, "You told me he started his Teaching on the Mount that day by making those distinctions:

'You have heard that it is said, but I tell you….' Right after his list of Beatitudes, correct?"

Simon nodded and added, "Yes. When he said he had come to fulfill the commandments, included in that is showing us the heart of the Sabbath. So, I have found these walks out in the countryside, sometimes lasting a couple of hours or more, bring me closer to the Master. But one day I decided to walk around Jerusalem instead of the countryside. It was different. It didn't feed my soul; it actually drained my soul.

"It was not that I was sinning by walking in the city, and I surely did not sense the Master's displeasure. But it was just the crowded nature of the city – the distractions that took me away *from* the Lord, not closer *to* him."

"I see," Saul said. "So perhaps I could just put it this way to my Gentile friends: Do not consider the Sabbath day of rest to be a burden, instead see it as a gift. You need the rest. We all do. And as for what you can do or not do on this day of rest: Do what feeds your soul, and brings you to the Lord. Do what soothes your soul. Consider what you are about to do as to whether it will bring you closer to the peace and contentment of the Lord, or away from him."

Saul hesitated, then continued, "I want to be sure they understand, it's not about what you can or cannot do; it's about what feeds your soul, and brings you closer to the Lord. Right?" Saul looked first at Peter and then at me.

SOUL REST

"Absolutely," I replied. "'To and From' clarifies the Sabbath command and frees it from a list of dos and don'ts. Jesus said it perfectly when he said,

> 'Come to me, all you who are weary and burdened, and I will give you rest. Take my yoke upon you and learn from me, for I am gentle and humble in heart,

and you will find rest for your souls. For my yoke is easy and my burden is light.'"

"I love that," Saul said, closing his eyes in contemplation. "Soul rest. Isn't that what we are all looking for?"

"I know I was, before I met Jesus," I said in agreement. "I just didn't know it. The Sabbath day of rest is one of God's surest paths to his soul rest."

Saul, the expert student of the Torah said, "Do you remember Jeremiah's words for the LORD?

"Stand at the crossroads and look;
ask for the ancient paths,
ask where the good way is, and walk in it,
and you will find rest for your souls."

I hesitated for a moment while we both mused over this, and then said, "One more thing, Saul. I know you recall Isaiah's beautiful comments about the Sabbath."

Saul nodded and said, "You are talking about,

'If you keep your feet from breaking the Sabbath
and from doing as you please on my holy day,
if you call the Sabbath a delight
and the LORD's holy day honorable,
and if you honor it by not going your own way
and not doing as you please or speaking idle words,
then you will find your joy in the LORD,
and I will cause you to ride on the heights of the land
and to feast on the inheritance of your father Jacob.'"

"Yes, isn't that just lovely?" I said, closing my eyes for a moment, taking in the rhythmic flow of the verses. "Do you notice he said, 'not doing as you please,' twice?"

Saul nodded. I continued, "I believe there are two truths here for us to take away:

"One: the Sabbath is not to be a day like any other day in which we do what suits us best. On this day, as a way to set it apart, I simply do not do anything I typically do the other six days of the week. It's interesting, isn't it, Saul, that, 'To make holy' means to set apart? I do not do just whatever comes to mind – 'doing as you please.' I want this day to be different than the other six – to be set apart unto itself."

"So when I honor the Sabbath I am set apart as well," Saul smiled with understanding.

I nodded and said, "This helps me establish a rhythm to my week. My life is no longer an endless cycle of work, eat and sleep. My weeks now have a soul-soothing rhythm to them."

I took a deep breath and continued, "Second: we are to call the Sabbath a delight. We are to enjoy the day. It is the Lord's Day, and we honor him by considering this day a delight, not a dread, as I used to.

"As you know Brother Saul, our Hebrew word for 'delight' carries a sense of luxury, as in delighting and luxuriating in a fine swath of silk. So when the Father tells us he wants us to delight in his day, he is saying he wants us to consider the Sabbath a day of pure joy, unlike the other six days. He wants us to feel the luxury of the Sabbath day of rest and reflection.

"He wants us to look forward to the Sabbath, and then to bathe ourselves in the precious presence of the Father, the Son and the Spirit."

Saul concluded our discussion with a smile and said, "Thank you both for clarifying this for me. To – from. Rest and reflection. Rejuvenation and reenergizing. Setting apart. Not just doing as I please. A gift. A delight. I am now confident I can explain this to my Gentile converts."

29

SONS OF THUNDER

John 10

After the Feast of Tabernacles we spent the fall months in Galilee. But soon enough it came time for the winter Feast of Hanukkah. This is our celebration of the victory of the Maccabees over the Greek Seleucids, about one hundred and seventy years before Jesus was born. This victory gave Israel her independence for eighty years and was in part why the zealots among us were sure we could – and should – overthrow the Romans among us.

These zealots were a fiery group who hated Rome, and were constantly agitating the Romans by assassinating soldiers and even civilians who were too cozy with the Romans. In a move that always surprised us, Jesus chose Simon the Zealot to be a part of the Twelve.

As we set off for Jerusalem, none of us could have imagined this would be our last trip from Galilee to Judah with Jesus. Unbeknownst to us, we were leaving Galilee with Jesus, not to return with him. Ever. Dr. Luke captures the mood perfectly:

> As the time approached for him to be taken up to heaven, Jesus resolutely set out for Jerusalem.

Yes, there was a resoluteness about Jesus that we had not seen before. He knew what we did not: that he was heading to his death. I will remind you of this fact: The cross did not happen to Jesus; Jesus happened to the cross. This was the start of his journey to death. And we the Twelve were following behind him, clueless as to what awaited us in the coming months.

To attest to just how clueless I was, Dr. Luke recorded what happened as we made our way from Galilee through Samaria:

> And he sent messengers on ahead, who went into a Samaritan village to get things ready for him; but the people there did not welcome him, because he was heading for Jerusalem. When the disciples James and John saw this, they asked, "Lord, do you want us to call fire down from heaven to destroy them?" But Jesus turned and rebuked them. Then he and his disciples went to another village.

James and I had walked into a Samaritan village ahead of Jesus and the other disciples. We were a little wary of the people, given the strained relationship between the Jews and the Samaritans. But we were brimming with confidence because we knew we had such good news for them. We were sure they would receive us with open arms.

But they did not. Before we even opened our mouths several of the village elders approached us with stern looks and asked us to leave immediately. We tried to maintain our composure, so I smiled and said, "Brothers, we know our people do not get along. But we are here to bring you the good news of the Kingdom of God!

"We want to tell you about the Messiah, Jesus ..."

But the elders interrupted me and said with derision, "Whose kingdom are you talking about Jew? Yours or ours? Get out! You are on your way to your precious Jerusalem – where you do not even welcome us. We don't want your kind around here!"

And with that one of them actually pushed me. Not hard, but big brother James almost jumped on him. I grabbed him and said, "Let's get out of here, brother. We will let the Master deal with these imbeciles."

Yes, your beloved disciple and teacher, Elder and Apostle John spoke that way. "Imbeciles." So we set out to find Jesus and told him what had happened. I blurted out in front the other disciples, red-faced and exasperated,

> "Lord, do you want us to call fire down from heaven to destroy them?"

There was an uncomfortable silence. Jesus looked at us with a puzzled look. Then he looked at the other disciples. He spoke sternly to us, reminding us of the many times he had healed Gentiles. And the many times he had used Samaritans as positive examples in his parables. I felt so foolish. I am sure my face was flushed.

From that time on, whenever James and I might be approaching Jesus and the other disciples, Jesus would stand up and with a huge smile and say, "Beware brothers, here come the Sons of Thunder!" He loved kidding us, and never missed an opportunity to do so. As I have already said, he had such a keen sense of humor. Peter would always laugh the hardest – I think because he was so glad someone else had done something boneheaded besides him.

Discipleship is a process where growth is seen through hardship and wrong turns. James and I had an episode that will demonstrate just how clueless one can be before the Holy Spirit begins to rule one's life.

SERVANT GREATNESS

Our mother, Salome, was close to Jesus' mother, Mary, and often traveled with us. She was with us as we were making our way toward Judea. One evening after we had eaten, mother called James and me aside and said, "I want to talk to the Master about your roles in his coming kingdom."

We had been thinking about this as well, although we never talked about it around the others. I am embarrassed to even tell you this story. James and I both eagerly agreed with Mother, so we waited until Jesus was alone and approached him. Mother kneeled down, and said she had a favor to ask him:

"What is it you want?" Jesus asked.

She said, "Grant that one of these two sons of mine may sit at your right and the other at your left in your kingdom."

Jesus contemplated her request for a moment, then looked at all three of us and said, "You don't know what you are asking. Can you drink the cup I am going to drink?"

"We can," we answered. (Of course, we did not know what cup or what it might mean.)

Jesus's eyes seemed to sadden as he quietly said, "You will indeed drink from my cup, but to sit at my right or left is not for me to grant. These places belong to those for whom they have been prepared by my Father."

He was not belittling us, nor was he rebuking us. He just stated this in a matter-of-fact manner, and then turned and moved away. One of the others overheard our conversation and told the other disciples. When the other ten heard about this, they were indignant with us. And they should have been. We were so blind back then.

Jesus called us all together and said, "You know that the rulers of the Gentiles lord it over them, and their high officials exercise authority over them. Not so with you. Instead, whoever wants to become great among you must be your servant, and whoever wants to be first must be your slave— just as the Son of

Man did not come to be served, but to serve, and to give his life as a ransom for many."

THE UPSIDE-DOWN REVERSAL

"Whoever wants to become great among you must be your servant, and whoever wants to be first must be your slave." I call this his Upside-Down Reversal. This was a constant theme in Jesus' teachings, and in the way he interacted with people. He had a special affection for the down and out. He never rushed past them. He always made time for them. He would sit patiently and listen to them. I mean really listen to them – not just to their words, but to what their hearts were saying. And they knew it. They knew he cared for them deeply.

For me it was a lesson I will never forget. The first shall be last and the last shall be first. It humbled me – always a good thing. And as Life in the Kingdom would have it, I would live out this Upside-Down Reversal not long after Jesus ascended to be with the Father.

After Stephen was stoned, a great persecution broke out against the church in Jerusalem, and all except the apostles were scattered throughout Judea and Samaria. Godly men buried Stephen and mourned deeply for him. But Saul began to destroy the church. Going from house to house, he dragged off both men and women and put them in prison.

Those who had been scattered preached the word wherever they went. Philip went down to a city in Samaria and proclaimed the Messiah there. When the crowds heard Philip and saw the signs he performed, they all paid close attention to what he said. For with shrieks, impure spirits came out of many, and many who were paralyzed or lame were healed. So there was great joy in that city.

When we heard that Samaria had accepted the word of God, Peter and I traveled to join Philip. When we arrived, we prayed for the new believers there, that they might receive the Holy

Spirit, because the Holy Spirit had not yet come on any of them. They had simply been baptized in the name of the Lord Jesus. Then Peter and I placed our hands on them, and they received the Holy Spirit.

What a joyous day that was. The Holy Spirit coming to the Samaritans! Just as Jesus had said,

> "But you will receive power when the Holy Spirit comes on you; and you will be my witnesses in Jerusalem, and in all Judea and Samaria, and to the ends of the earth."

But for me it was especially poignant, and especially meaningful. You see, this took place not far from the village that had turned James and me away. And here we were, preaching Jesus to these same people, and laying on hands for the Holy Spirit. Talk about an Upside-Down Reversal!

In my old Self, I wanted to call down lightning and thunder on these people. And now I am calling down the great Spirit of God. Indeed, the first shall be last and the last shall be first.

After this episode, Jesus led us into the region of Judea to the other side of the Jordan, away from the Samaritan territory. But we would soon find ourselves in a contentious stand-off with the Jewish authorities, as the pressure mounted on them, due to Jesus' increasing popularity.

30

MARTHA

Luke 10

Then came the Festival of Dedication (Hanukkah) at Jerusalem. It was winter, and Jesus was in the temple courts walking in Solomon's Colonnade. The Jewish authorities were gathered around him, saying, "How long will you keep us in suspense? If you are the Messiah, tell us plainly."

Rest assured they were not asking this for information. They were not asking to hear Jesus declare, "I am the long-awaited Messiah!" No, they wanted to expose this popular rabbi as a phony.

Jesus was not threatened and certainly saw through their motives. He answered, "I did tell you, but you do not believe. The works I do in my Father's name testify about me, but you do not believe because you are not my sheep. My sheep listen to my voice; I know them, and they follow me. I give them eternal life, and they shall never perish; no one will snatch them out of my hand. My Father, who has given them to me, is greater than all; no one can snatch them out of my Father's hand. I and the Father are one."

This infuriated the Jewish authorities because Jesus was calling himself God. Again his Jewish opponents picked up stones to stone him, but Jesus said to them, "I have shown you many good works from the Father. For which of these do you stone me?"

"We are not stoning you for any good work," they replied, "but for blasphemy, because you, a mere man, claim to be God."

As blind as they were, they could at least see that Jesus was indeed claiming to be God. This is a fact many overlook. Many people want to take Jesus as a wonderful and wise teacher. Others think of him as a prophet of God. And still others just think of him as this kind and compassionate, itinerant rabbi - one whose message of love and mercy and forgiveness is something we should all try to emulate.

But Jesus did not leave us this option. He was sure not to. He made it clear to these important men, and to many others, that he was the Messiah. He was the Son of God. So we must choose. We either consider him to be a deceitful swindler or a lunatic. Or we take him at his word, that he is the Son of God. Let us dispense with all other options. Either ignore him or fall at his feet and surrender to him as your Lord. But none of this lukewarm, halfhearted stuff.

After this, Jesus took us back across the Jordan River to the place where John had been baptizing in the early days. There he stayed, and many people came to him. They said, "Though John never performed a sign, all that John said about this man was true." And in that place many surrendered and put their trust in Jesus.

We stayed around the Jordan for a few weeks. The weather was warmer here and we all enjoyed this respite from the conflict and tension in Jerusalem. Jesus seemed at ease here and spoke about his cousin John the Baptizer often. It was almost as if he was reliving those early days before the Jewish authorities' opposition became so confrontational.

But soon we got word that our friend Lazarus was sick. He was from Bethany, the village of Mary and her sister Martha. (This Mary, whose brother Lazarus now lay sick, was the same one who poured perfume on the Lord and wiped his feet with her hair.) So the sisters sent word to Jesus, "Lord, the one you love is sick."

BUSY AND DISTRACTED

You may remember Jesus' dear friends, Lazarus, Martha and Mary. They lived in Bethany. Jesus loved all three equally, but he seemed to truly relish his time with Lazarus, the brother. I think he felt like he could just sit and be himself with Lazarus. Lazarus' home was quiet, and the two of them would often sit all afternoon just talking about the Scriptures. Lazarus asked many deep questions, questions I would never have even thought to ask. Jesus relished this back and forth and would ask Lazarus challenging questions in return.

That kind of give-and-take debate gave Jesus great joy.

Their conversations, and sometimes debates, could go on for hours. The younger sister, Mary, would sit near them and listen to all they said, absorbing Jesus' words deep into her heart. She had such a peaceful way about her. Neither she nor Lazarus ever seemed to be in a hurry, and Mary would not let anything distract her from listening intently to Jesus.

On one occasion we had all gathered at their home for a meal. Martha prepared and served the meal. She was a woman who could not just sit still. Martha was just the opposite of Mary. Don't get me wrong, she was a pleasant person, friendly and welcoming. She loved to have Jesus visit and would always prepare great meals for us. The twelve of us loved it when Jesus said we were stopping in Bethany!

But Martha could be difficult. She would get distracted by all the preparations that had to be made. I remember this occasion vividly. She had worked herself into a frenzy cleaning the house and getting the food ready. When she got into this mode, I would be sure to stay out of her way. I had been bossed around by Martha before, and even snapped at when I did not do something the way she wanted it done.

Mary typically got the brunt of Martha's frustrations. I have no doubt Martha considered Mary lazy. And she certainly thought of her as inefficient, and a time-waster. Martha reminded me of ... me, back in my fishing days: rushed, hurried, and harried, temper rising and patience evaporating. Distracted by all my important activities.

I was watching her get worked up. I elbowed James in the side and said, "Watch out. Martha is getting frustrated." James looked her way and saw her face reddening and quietly walked outside. So did Nathanael and Philip. They knew better than to get in the way of Martha when she was pressing and stressing.

I saw her finally set down her bowl, and march over to Jesus and Lazarus. She came to Jesus and cried out, "Lord, don't you care that my sister has left me to do the work by myself? Tell her to help me!"

I have to say, I was trying my best to suppress a smile. Poor Martha. She was, after all, doing all the work. She was hot, she was weary, and she was tired. But the truth is she actually liked being this way. She thrived on being busy. Some of us had tried before to help her out, but she pushed us out of the way, murmuring, "If you want something done right, you have to do it yourself."

Can you relate?

BE STILL AND KNOW THAT I AM GOD

On this particular day Jesus had told Martha not to busy herself preparing a meal. We had brought with us fresh bread and even some honey and dates. Jesus wanted her to relax and just sit with him, and listen to what he had to say.

But Martha did not want to just sit. She did not like *just sitting*. As a matter of fact, I do not think I ever saw her just being still. She could not, don't you see? Busyness made her happy. Busyness made her feel important. She was accomplishing things! Busyness made her feel needed – and busyness made her feel ... necessary.

Busyness defined her, and she liked it that way.

I have to pause and ask you, you reading this now, does this sound a little too familiar?

Martha simply could not sit still. She was distracted and disjointed and miserable as she complained to Jesus. And she was about to make everyone else miserable. This is often the way of busy people. No one can really relax around them. Jesus glanced at Martha with a look, not unlike the look he gave James and me after we wanted to call down thunder and lightning on that Samaritan village.

He loved Martha and was not in the least bit irritated with her. But he was also saddened because he knew that with all her busyness, she was missing the really important things in life. Martha knew a lot about Jesus. She had spent time around him. But she did not know Jesus as Mary knew him. Mary, as well as Lazarus - had a deeper knowledge of Jesus – a relationship that penetrated her heart.

Mary's relationship was personal and visceral. Martha's was surface – sincere, but still surface.

ONLY ONE THING

Jesus turned to Martha and said, "Martha, Martha, you are worried and upset about many things, but only one thing is needed. Look at Mary. She sits here quietly, listening to what I am saying. She is soaking in my words, but you are too busy and distracted to spend time with me. Mary has chosen what is better, and it will not be taken away from her."

Martha did indeed look at Mary, but it was with a frown.

"But you my dear, sweet friend," Jesus continued with a smile, "are missing the things that are truly important." He paused, and then said, "Martha, do you remember King David's psalm?"

Martha looked at Jesus and said, "Some, my Lord. But which one are you referring to?"

Jesus closed his eyes and replied,

"'One thing I ask from the LORD,
this only do I seek:
that I may dwell in the house of the LORD
all the days of my life,
to gaze on the beauty of the LORD
and to seek him in his temple.'"

Jesus then said to Martha, "You are worried about so many things, but only one thing is needed. I want you to just be still for a while. Come, sit down next to me."

Jesus smiled with his warm, infectious smile, and opened his arms toward Martha. I watched her as she initially began to turn back toward her food, but then she stopped, hesitated, and slowly turned and sat down next to Jesus. Her beet-red face softened as Jesus patted her on her shoulder.

He then looked directly into her eyes with love and affection and said, "Good. Now, just be still and know that I am God."

"Only one thing is needed," Jesus said to Martha. For Martha, and for you and for me, this *one thing* is to go deeper in our relationship with Jesus. Everything else is periphery. All your good activities; all those things that "if I don't do them, who will?"- all your religious service – they mean nothing if you are not getting to know your Savior personally, intimately.

Only one thing. Just the two of you. You and Jesus.

The value of our public service for God flows from our private intimacy with him. I must remember this over and over. Trust me. I, too, can get busy and distracted, and lose sight of the

Holy Spirit. I, too, can be distracted by all that has to get done, and bypass my time alone with my Lord.

It's hard to be still when there is so much to be done. And harder still when I think I am the one to get it all done!

31

FOUR DAY FAITH

John 11

Now back to Lazarus. Martha and Mary sent word to us, "Lord, the one you love, your dear friend and brother, is sick."

When he heard this, Jesus said, "This sickness will not end in death. No, it is for God's glory, so that God's Son may be glorified through it. This will reveal the greatness of the Son of God by what takes place."

This is what "to glorify" means: to accurately reveal who God is and how he does things.

Even though Jesus loved Mary, Martha, and Lazarus deeply, we remained where we were by the Jordan for two more days. This was confusing to us. Why would he wait? It made no sense. We knew he could heal Lazarus from anywhere -- he did not need to be at his side. But still, not to go immediately to be with the family he loved so much was a disconnect for us.

But at this point Jesus was withdrawing a bit from us. It was as if he knew something we did not know, and it troubled his soul. He was resolute; he was clearly on a mission, but he was also struggling against something, or someone, and we could not relate.

Finally, on the third day, Jesus walked over to us and said, "Come. It's time to go to Bethany."

"But Teacher," Nathaniel said, perplexed, as we all were, "do you really want to go back there? It was just a short time ago the Jewish authorities of Judea were going to stone you!"

Jesus looked around at us and replied, "Are there not twelve hours of daylight in every day? You can go through a day without the fear of stumbling when you walk with the One who gives light to the world. But you will stumble when the light is not in you, for you'll be walking in the dark."

I remembered his words back at the Feast of Tabernacles, "I am the light of the world. Whoever follows me will never walk in darkness, but will have the light of life." But I was still not registering his meaning. This was all so bewildering.

We were confused by his words, and Jesus could see that we were. So he went on to tell us, "Lazarus, our friend, has just fallen asleep. It's time that I go and awaken him."

Peter was becoming frustrated and replied, "Lord, if he sleeps, he will get better." Of course Jesus had been speaking of his death, but we were so dumbfounded we thought he meant natural sleep.

Then Jesus made it plain to us, "Lazarus is dead. And for your sake, I'm glad I wasn't there, because now you have another opportunity to see who I am, so you will learn to truly trust in me. Come, let's go and see him."

Now we were all totally confused that Jesus had waited for Lazarus to die. What was his plan? And why would we go back into the valley of the shadow of death – where we knew the Jewish authorities were waiting to try to kill him – and possibly us, too?

But Thomas (also known as Didymus because he was a twin) shrugged his shoulders and said to the rest of us, "Let us also go, that we may die with him." I know Thomas is often referred to as "Doubting Thomas," because he would not initially accept Jesus' resurrection, but you should know he was anything but. He was one of our stronger disciples, and he was not afraid to die with Jesus.

This was the kick in the pants we needed, so we packed up our belongings and headed up the desert hills through Jericho, to Bethany, on the Mount of Olives.

PERFECT LOVE DRIVES OUT ALL FEAR

Now when we arrived at Bethany, which was only about two miles from Jerusalem, Jesus found that Lazarus had already been in the tomb for four days. This was on purpose – something the Master had planned. He was going to send a message to everyone, especially the Sanhedrin.

The message was: "I Am! And I am here to stay."

Lazarus being dead four days is significant. It is precisely why Jesus waited two days. You see in our culture we believed the soul, the *nephesh,* hovered near the body for three days after death. But by the fourth day the nephesh departed - and with it all hope of any revival.

Recall Jesus had sent the messenger from Martha and Mary with this message:

> "This sickness will not end in death for Lazarus, but will bring glory and praise to God. This will reveal the greatness of the Son of God by what takes place."

They would have received this message with hope and confidence on the day Lazarus died, assuming Jesus would soon arrive and revive Lazarus. After all, he had raised the widow's son at Nain, and Jairus' daughter from the dead, and he could do that for Lazarus. Recall his words to Jairus and the other mourners:

"Stop wailing," Jesus said. "She is not dead but asleep."

They laughed at him, knowing that she was dead. But he took her by the hand and said, "My child, get up!" Her spirit – her nephesh - returned, and at once she stood up.

"Her spirit returned." This is exactly what the sisters would have been expecting: Jesus would arrive and all would be well. But he did not arrive. Not that day, nor the next, nor the next. Not until the fourth day.

Martha and Mary could have remained hopeful during those first three days, because the nephesh would still be hovering around. It would be a fantastic miracle, but they knew Jesus could do it. But as we arrived on the fourth day, all hope was gone. Their faith, although not shattered, was certainly strained to the breaking point.

Are you beginning to see why Jesus waited those two days back across the Jordan? Again, he stated his purpose plainly:

> "This sickness will not end in death for Lazarus, but will bring glory and praise to God. This will reveal the greatness of the Son of God by what takes place."

Jesus wanted us all to see he had power over death, even a four-day death. He wanted us all to see death was impotent in the face of his power and his purpose – and his perfect love. He was going to glorify his Heavenly Father – to accurately reveal who he is, what he cares about, and how he does things.

Over these years I have had my trust tested beyond the first or second, or even the third day. Perhaps a one-day faith could be normal for a follower of Jesus. And as I grew in my trust of the Master's purpose, his presence, his power and his perfect love, my trust grew in strength. But when I found myself in a four-day faith situation, my trust wavered.

In those four-day-faith situations my feelings would start to take over, and that dreaded sense of hopelessness would raise its sordid head. In these times, as I have mentioned previously, I must return to the facts:

He is perfectly present with me.

He is perfectly powerful.

Jesus loves me perfectly.

And remember, "Perfect love drives out all fear."
As he declared to us,

> "Are not two sparrows sold for a penny? Yet not one of them will fall to the ground apart from your Father's will. And even the very hairs of your head are all numbered. So don't be afraid; you are worth more than many sparrows."

SATAN'S 3 DS

Satan wants you to lose hope. He wants to destroy your faith – cripple your trust in Jesus. So in these 1 and 2 and 3 and even 4 day trials of faith, Satan begins to plant distracting and discouraging thoughts in our heads. Thoughts such as, "Okay, maybe you think Jesus has been there for you before, but that was just a coincidence. And even if he was that time, this time he won't show up for you."

Destroy, distract, discourage. If he can keep you out of a relationship with Jesus, he will have destroyed your soul. This is his chief goal. But if he loses that battle, and you are born again, he will spend the rest of your life trying to destroy the "Life to the full," Jesus came to give you. He will do this by distracting you and discouraging you.

But you can stop him. Yes, you have the power - Holy Spirit power - to rebuke Satan and run him off. Simon Peter stated this plainly in his first letter:

> Be alert and of sober mind. Your enemy the devil prowls around like a roaring lion looking for someone to devour. Resist him, standing firm in the faith, because you know that the family of believers throughout the world is undergoing the same kind of sufferings.

James said it like this:

> Submit yourselves, then, to God. Resist the devil, and he will flee from you. Come near to God and he will come near to you.

I want you to know that I am not afraid of Satan. He has no power over me. I do not seek a confrontation with him, but I am certainly not afraid of him. And I do not want you, my child, to be afraid of him either. Why? Because,

> The spirit of the antichrist, which you have heard is coming and even now is already in the world. You, dear children, are from God and have overcome them, because the one who is in you is greater than the one who is in the world.

The Master was stretching and strengthening Martha and Mary's trust, and he will do the same for you. He loves you that much. He loves you just as you are, but too much to leave you as you are. You, too, can have this four-day-faith.

32

LAZARUS COME OUT!

John 11

Many friends of Mary and Martha had come from the area to console them over the loss of their brother. When Martha heard that Jesus was approaching the village, she slipped away from the mourners and went out to meet him. But Mary stayed in the house.

As Martha approached us, tears flowing from her eyes, she stopped in front of Jesus. For a moment she just looked at him. Then she dropped her eyes and said to Jesus, "My Lord, if only you had come sooner, my brother wouldn't have died. But I know that if you were to ask God for anything, he would do it for you."

Jesus stepped toward Martha, gently lifted her chin to look her in the eyes, and said, "Your brother will rise and live."

She dried her tears, brushed her hair back and replied, "Yes, I know he will rise with everyone else on resurrection day."

"Martha," Jesus said, compassion pouring out from his heart, "You don't have to wait until then. I am the Resurrection, and I am the Life Eternal." He paused and smiled, and continued, "Anyone who clings to me in faith, anyone who surrenders to me and places his trust in me, even though he dies physically, will live forever. And the one who lives by trusting in me will actually never die. Do you believe this?"

(Remember, Jesus was not asking Martha for his own information, he wanted her to look deeply into her own heart. He wanted her to move beyond "believing in Jesus," and learn to believe what he believed.)

Then Martha straightened up, stood a little taller and replied, "Yes, Lord, I do. I've always believed that you are the Anointed One, the Son of God, who has come into the world for us." Then she left and hurried off to her sister, Mary. She called her aside from all the mourners and whispered to her, "The Master is here and he's asking for you."

When Mary heard this, she quickly went off to find him, for Jesus was lingering outside the village at the same spot where Martha had met him. Now when Mary's friends who were comforting her noticed how quickly she ran out of the house, they followed her, assuming she was going to the tomb of her brother to mourn there.

When Mary finally found Jesus outside the village, she fell at his feet in tears and said, "Lord, if only you had been here, my brother would not have died."

When Jesus looked at Mary and saw her weeping at his feet, and all her friends who were with her grieving, he shuddered with emotion and was deeply moved with tenderness and compassion. I cannot say exactly why, but it seemed he was brokenhearted over the hold death had over his beloved friends. I was watching him closely. His mood was other-worldly. I do not know how to describe it for you. His countenance was downcast, and his face was a mixture of sadness, frustration, pity, and even anger.

I had not seen Jesus this way before, and the only other time I would see him in this agitated state was in the Garden of Gethsemane, when he sweated blood.

He said to them, "Where did you bury him?"

"Lord, come with us and we'll show you," they replied.

I saw tears spilling down Jesus' face. This was terribly disconcerting to all of us. Peter and James exchanged looks of concern, Matthew and Thomas shuffled their feet nervously, and Andrew stepped closer to me. He whispered, "John, what is going on? Is Jesus alright? Can we help him in any way?" I shrugged and shook my head, my eyes meeting his and then dropping down to the ground.

As I have reflected on Jesus' crying that day, it seems he was distressed at the terrible hold death had over the human race. It may also be that he wept at the misery of death we humans – his Father's beloved creation – suffer because we have failed to believe him when he said:

> "Very truly I tell you, whoever obeys my word will never see death."

So I will ask you, just as Jesus asked Martha, "Do you believe this?"

Do you actually believe what Jesus believed?

> "I am the resurrection and the life. The one who believes in me will live, even though they die; and whoever lives by believing in me will never die. Do you believe this?"

Seeing Jesus weep caused many of the mourners to say, "Look how much he loved Lazarus." Yet others said, "Isn't this the One who opens blind eyes? Why didn't he do something to keep Lazarus from dying?"

DEEP CALLING DEEP

Clouds were forming over us and the sky was darkening. The wind picked up. I felt a chill in my bones. Then Jesus, with intense emotion, came to the tomb—a cave with a stone placed over its entrance. We were following at a distance, not at all sure we wanted to see what might come next. Jesus' eyes swept the crowd as he told them, "Roll away the stone."

Then Martha whispered, "But Lord, it's been four days since he died—by now his body is already decomposing. The smell will be terrible!"

Jesus looked at her, his eyes penetrating into hers, and said,

> "Didn't I tell you that if you will believe in me, surrender to me, and transfer your trust from yourself, to me and to my Kingdom, you will see God unveil his power?"

Martha stepped back and held Mary's arm tightly. They braced themselves together, their eyes darting back and forth furtively.

The men rolled away the heavy stone. Jesus gazed into heaven and said, "Father, thank you that you have heard my prayer, for you listen to every word I speak. Now, so that these who stand here with me will believe that you have sent me to the earth as your messenger, I will use the Holy Spirit's power you have given me."

Then, with a loud voice Jesus shouted with authority: "Lazarus! Come out of the tomb!"

There was a moment, a stillness, a look from Jesus into the very darkness of the tomb. Then a light flashed from within. I saw it and felt a stirring in my soul. There was some kind of communication going on between Jesus and the spirit world, but not with words. It was deep calling unto deep.

Then in front of everyone, Lazarus, who had died four days earlier, slowly hobbled out. He still had grave clothes tightly wrapped around his hands and feet and covering his face. I almost stumbled as I unintentionally backed away. A hush fell across the crowd, a blanket of silence. A woman gasped. Peter held his breath. James looked as if he had seen a ghost.

Jesus said to them, "Unwrap him and let him loose."

The sun suddenly broke through. Mary and Martha rushed to Lazarus and together they pulled the linens off his body. Lazarus was left wearing only an undergarment, but no one cared. The energy was as powerful as a lightning storm. The joy was overflowing. The sisters kept kissing their dear brother and exclaiming, "You are back! You are back!" They looked back to Jesus, wild wonder in their eyes, then started kissing Lazarus again and saying, "We love you so much! Please never leave us again!"

The people were clapping and singing praise songs. The men were belting out "Hallelujahs" boisterously and slapping each other on the back, while the women hugged everyone in sight.

In the midst of the celebration, I noticed Lazarus look at Jesus. Their eyes connected. No words were spoken. None needed to be. It was the purest example of deep calling unto deep I have ever experienced. As their eyes held each other's gaze, Jesus nodded his head slightly. Lazarus did the same.

Shortly after that Lazarus, Martha and Mary fell to the ground, knocked over by pure joy. What a sight it was! Jesus' seventh and final sign. A sign that stated clearly, "I Am, and I am here to stay."

My dear friend and prophet, John bar John, perfectly captures this encounter:

> Here is the final and most dramatic of the seven signs: Jesus engages death itself, that dreaded moment we all fear. Here we get to hear the strongest and most winsome of all the "I am sayings," when Jesus speaks to Mary in the cavern of her grief: "I am

the resurrection and the life. Whoever believes in me, though he die, yet shall he live…"

There is a gold mine of riches here, but notice three quick things:

It seems beyond odd that Jesus would hear that his friend Lazarus was standing on the brow overlooking death, and Jesus not only does not react with expected immediacy to stride the miles to his side, instead he waits. You sense a strange, unfrantic purposefulness in Jesus.

There is something of the glory of God and resurrection and a brilliant victory coming; but is it not agonizing, heartbreaking in the waiting? Looking backward through the resurrection, here is a hard learning: Jesus does not move on the groove of our expectations; he does not rush, does not junk his immediate agenda to heal Lazarus.

But the finale brings us to an empty tomb in Bethany with a raised Lazarus—a joy which exceeds our expectations. Are you in school here with the two sisters? Are you learning that Heaven's clock is different from ours? Can you look back at crises and see that God was "working the night shift," silently, relentlessly, unobserved, with a coming victory on the other side?

The most moving of all the "I am" sayings is present tense. "I am the resurrection and the life…" He does not say, "Some day I might bring resurrection." When we are in Christ, when he had landed within us and done that second birth, when we shipwreck at his feet in trust, we enter eternal life.

Martha thought that someday, some vague day over the hill, "there might be heaven." Think about it. Jesus is not the giver of victory in some obscure future. He is the victory of life over death in the rugged heartbreak of the present. Do you believe that? Can you taste that? What do you believe?

There are more unforgettable words here. At the tomb in Bethany, as the friends unbind Lazarus, Jesus says "Unbind him and let him go." That final verb (*aphesis*) which Jesus offers Lazarus as gift, means *set him free*; leave it behind; escape this prison. It also is the word used when the steward of a horse race sets the horses loose.

"Go!" and there they gallop down the track. There's a new explosive gift of life here, nothing somber. Jesus cries in a loud voice (so that if there are others back in Lazarus' tomb they may hear; that we may hear it as well): Send him off! He doesn't belong to the grave anymore!

33

OUR LAST SUPPER

It was just before the Passover Festival. Jesus knew that the hour had come for him to leave this world and go to the Father. Having loved his own who were in the world, he loved them to the end.

The evening meal was in progress, and the devil had already prompted Judas, the son of Simon Iscariot, to betray Jesus. Jesus knew that the Father had put all things under his power, and that he had come from God and was returning to God; so he got up from the meal, took off his outer clothing, and wrapped a towel around his waist. After that, he poured water into a basin and began to wash his disciples' feet, drying them with the towel that was wrapped around him.

We were all dumbfounded. What was Jesus doing? This menial task of washing our dusty feet should be done by a servant. Certainly not the host. I wanted to reach out to stop Jesus. But none of us could move. We were held in place by a power far beyond us. Jesus went to each of the twelve, slowly, methodically, dipping the rag in the water basin and washing the dust off our dirty feet.

He came to Simon Peter, who said to him, "Lord, are you going to wash my feet?" Simon was pulling his feet away from Jesus, a look of dismay on his face.

Jesus held his gaze for a moment, then replied, "You do not realize now what I am doing, but later you will understand."

Peter stood and backed away from Jesus and said, "No, Master," said Peter, "you shall never wash my feet." Jesus simply replied, "Unless I wash you, you have no part with me." "Then, Lord," Simon Peter replied, sitting back down on the floor, "not just my feet but my hands and my head as well!"

Jesus looked up, and then allowing his eyes to fall on each one of us answered, "Those who have had a bath need only to wash their feet; their whole body is clean. And you are clean, though not every one of you." For he knew who was going to betray him, and that was why he said not everyone was clean.

When he had finished washing our feet, he put on his clothes and returned to his place.

"Do you understand what I have done for you?" he asked them, looking at Simon. "You call me 'Teacher' and 'Lord,' and rightly so, for that is what I am. Now that I, your Lord and Teacher, have washed your feet, you also should wash one another's feet."

I am sorry to have to admit this but none of us were the least bit interested in being a servant, especially if it meant washing dirty feet.

> "I have set you an example that you should do as I have done for you. Very truly I tell you, no servant is greater than his master, nor is a messenger greater than the one who sent him. The greatest among you will be your servant. For those who exalt themselves will be humbled, and those who humble themselves will be exalted. Now that you know these things, you will be blessed if you do them."

We all looked at each other and nodded, although we really did not understand what he meant. After he had said this, Jesus looked away from us and seemed to be struggling to hold it together. He was troubled in spirit and testified, "Very truly I tell you, one of you is going to betray me."

We stared at one another, at a loss to know which of us he meant. I was sitting next to Jesus, reclining on his right. Simon Peter motioned to me and whispered, "Ask him which one he means."

Leaning back against Jesus, I asked him, "Lord, who is it?"

Jesus answered, "It is the one to whom I will give this piece of bread when I have dipped it in the dish." Then, dipping the piece of bread, he gave it to Judas, who was reclining on Jesus' left. As soon as Judas took the bread, Satan entered into him.

So Jesus told him, "What you are about to do, do quickly." But no one at the meal understood why Jesus said this to him. Since Judas had charge of the money, I assumed Jesus was telling him to buy what was needed for the festival, or to give something to the poor. As soon as Judas had taken the bread, he went out.

And suddenly it was night.

There are many sublayers to that night, but allow me to spend a few moments explaining the seating arrangement, and what it tells us about Jesus' intent.

When Jesus said, "The greatest among you will be your servant," he was further indicating he would not be conquering with might. And neither would we. 'Might' in the Kingdom of God is through love, sacrifice, serving and surrender – with an emphasis on serving. Remember the lesson from the young woman caught in adultery: Power down, not power up.

TRICLINIUM TABLE SEATING ARRANGEMENTS

The most subtle aspect of the dinner that night was the seating arrangement. This might escape some people's eyes, but a quick explanation of what the table looked like, and how Jesus seated us around it, will shed clarifying light.

We were sitting at a triclinium table. This is a low sitting table arranged in three parts, forming a "U" shape. We reclined, as in lying on our left side and eating with our right hands, as we reached across to pick up the bread and stew. This was typical of dinners such as this seder meal. Here is a picture to help:

Jesus was sitting in the host's seat. He had me sit to his right, which was the seat of the host's 'right-hand man.' Jesus placed Judas to his left, which was the Guest of Honor's seat. Are you beginning to see the subtle layers? Placing Judas in this seat of honor was surprising, but Peter's seat was stupefying.

Jesus seated him in the … servant's seat.

For a reason. It was as if Jesus was speaking directly to Peter when he said,

> "The greatest among you will be your servant. For those who exalt themselves will be humbled, and those who humble themselves will be exalted."

Jesus knew Peter was going to be our leader after he returned to Heaven. He also knew Peter would fail miserably if he tried to lead with his own strength. Peter was a can-do, "I will get it done," power up kind of man. He lived under the mantra, "If it is to be, it is up to me. If I don't, then it won't."

Jesus knew that for Peter, "What works at work," was not going to work in his coming Kingdom among us. So he started the night by seating Peter in the conspicuous spot of the servant's seat. I can tell you Simon was both embarrassed, and furious – and humiliated. Red-faced and red-hot tempered. We talked many times later about that night - how he resented me being in the right-hand man's seat, and how he loathed Judas being in the Guest of Honor seat.

However, Jesus was sifting Simon. He stated as much:

> "Simon, Simon, Satan has asked to sift all of you as wheat. But I have prayed for you, Simon, that your faith may not fail. And when you have turned back, strengthen your brothers."

Simon told me later he was assuming Jesus would say, "But I have prayed for you, Simon, ... and therefore I will not allow Satan to sift you." But of course that is not what Jesus would pray for. He knew Simon, with all his self-confidence and bombastic personality, would need sifting. He would need Self, his greatest enemy, as well as ours, sifted off him as chaff sifted from the wheat at the threshing floor.

And why? Because the greater the pride, and Self, the greater the need for sifting. Yet again, it is all about surrendering.

The deeper the Surrender the lighter the sifting.

The lighter the Surrender the deeper the sifting.

The longer it takes to surrender the longer the sifting.

And as long as we resist surrendering, as Jesus said, "Truly I tell you, you will not get out until you have paid the last penny."

One more point about Peter's servant's seat. Seated in that seat, as the servant for the night, he was supposed to wash everyone's feet. Before Jesus stood up to begin the foot washing, I noticed he stared at Simon for a moment. It was as if he was saying, "Are you going to do this? Because if you won't, if you are too proud, I will." Simon returned Jesus' look with a glare, then dropped his eyes and stared at the floor.

So as Jesus slowly went around the table, the tension mounting as he methodically dipped the rag into the wash basin, and then washed each disciple's feet, Peter's face was turning beet red. This is why he refused Jesus washing his feet. He was beside himself; it was all too much. And he was right where Jesus wanted him.

Over all these years, Jesus' washing of our feet echoes in my memory, as do his words,

> Everything they (The Pharisees) do is done for people to see: They make their phylacteries wide and the tassels on their garments long; they love the place of honor at banquets and the most important seats in the synagogues.
>
> "When someone invites you to a wedding feast, do not take the place of honor, for a person more distinguished than you may have been invited. If so, the host who invited both of you will come and say to you, 'Give this person your seat.' Then, humiliated, you will have to take the least important place.
>
> "But when you are invited, take the lowest place, so that when your host comes, he will say to you, 'Friend, move up to a better place.' Then you will be honored in the presence of all the other guests. For all those who exalt themselves will be humbled, and those who humble themselves will be exalted."

My only explanation for Jesus seating Judas in the Guest of Honor seat was to indicate to his betrayer – and to us, "I know what you are about to do, and I love you anyway."

Isn't this what Jesus meant when he told us just a moment later,

> "A new command I give you: Love one another. As I have loved you, so you must love one another. By this everyone will know that you are my disciples, if you love one another."

And in his Sermon on the Mount, when he said,

> "You have heard that it was said, 'Love your neighbor and hate your enemy.' But I tell you, love your enemies and pray for those who persecute you, that you may be children of your Father in heaven."

Jesus was living out his teaching right there for us to see. We couldn't understand it that night, but after the Holy Spirit invaded our hearts, rest assured, none of us ever forgot it.

34

THE UPPER ROOM DISCOURSE

John 14 – 17

There are so many things Jesus said to us that night I would like to share with you. I have recorded all the details in my gospel account. I hope you will read them there. But here, I want to share with you Jesus' focus on the Holy Spirit. Because, as he said,

> "Very truly I tell you, whoever believes in me will do the works I have been doing, and they will do even greater things than these, because I am going to the Father. But very truly I tell you, it is for your good that I am going away. Unless I go away, the Advocate – the Holy Spirit - will not come to you; but if I go, I will send him to you."

Now that is an astounding statement! We would be better off with the Holy Spirit than with Jesus? How could this be? And we would do even greater things than what Jesus did? This made no sense to us at the time. How could it? We had no conception of the divine power and presence of the Holy Spirit

Jesus knew what we could not know that night: That everything that would happen to us, and through us, after his departure, would be powered by the Holy Spirit. He would later state emphatically,

> "But you will receive power when the Holy Spirit comes on you; and you will be my witnesses in Jerusalem, and in all Judea and Samaria, and to the ends of the earth."

Everything Jesus said that night was to comfort us, to guide us, and to prepare us for life after his departure. He began by saying,

> "Do not let your hearts be troubled. You believe in God; believe also in me. My Father's house - his bet 'ab ... his family compound - has many rooms; if that were not so, would I have told you that I am going there to prepare a place for you? And if I go and prepare a place for you, I will come back and take you to be with me that you also may be where I am."

As he continued his comforting words he said,

> "I will not leave you orphaned. I'm coming back. In just a little while the world will no longer see me, but you're going to see me because I am alive and you're about to come alive. At that moment you will know absolutely that I'm in my Father, and you're in me, and I'm in you."

"Because I am alive, and you're about to come alive." He was speaking of our Feast of Shavuot. (The Gentiles and the Greeks call it Pentecost.) That is the day when the Holy Spirit arrived and lit us on fire with his power. Yes, we came alive, fully alive, on that Shavuot day, with a power and a force we had only briefly experienced when Jesus sent us out on our two missionary trips.

By the way, the Jews celebrate God's two greatest gifts each year in Jerusalem with these feasts:

1. Passover – The gift of their freedom
2. Shavuot/Pentecost (fifty days after Passover) – The gift of God's instructions and teachings for life

But for followers of Jesus, the gifts of Passover and Pentecost happen on the same day – the day you are born again. On that day you are freed from slavery and you are given the Holy Spirit.

Are you celebrating the two greatest gifts God could ever give you?

1. The day he delivered you from your slavery to sin, as well as your slavery to your Self – (Self: that most evil and tyrannical slave driver.)
2. The gift of his Holy Spirit, who gives you the power to remain free from the slavery of your Self, and to have the power to live the life that is truly life.

May you remember and celebrate your personal Passover/Pentecost each year. Make a big deal out of it because it is a big deal. But more poignantly, have you experienced a personal deliverance from the slavery of sin and Self? Ask yourself; challenge yourself; do not just sluff this off. The stakes are too high.

That last night we could not process his words about the Holy Spirit - the eyes of our hearts had not yet been enlightened. We were not yet to the point where we believed everything Jesus believed. But thankfully he promised us the Holy Spirit would remind us of all he said and did:

> "All this I have spoken while still with you. But the Advocate, the Holy Spirit, whom the Father will send in my name, will teach you all things and will remind you of everything I have said to you."
>
> "If you love me, keep my commands. And I will ask the Father, and he will give you another advocate to help you and be with you forever - the Spirit of truth. The world cannot accept him, because it neither sees him nor knows him. But you know him, for he lives with you and will be in you."

As we prepared to leave the upper room and walk over to the Mount of Olives, Jesus assured us again,

> "Peace I leave with you; my peace I give you. I do not give to you as the world gives. Do not let your hearts be troubled and do not be afraid. Come now; let us leave."

FRUIT AND VINES

As we passed through the Eastern (Golden) Gate, I pondered the words of Jesus, and this Advocate about which he spoke. He talked as if this Spirit was a 'he,' as in a person. The stars were brilliant that night, and the cool air helped revive me after our long Seder Passover meal. The night was so quiet and beautiful, crisp and clear. Surely some of the things Jesus said about his impending death could not be true. Not tonight.

I was lost in my reverie when we found ourselves in a small vineyard. Jesus bent down and lifted up a vine off the ground and said,

> "I am the true vine, and my Father is the gardener. He lifts up and cleans off every branch in me that bears no fruit, while every branch that does bear fruit

> he prunes, so that it will be even more fruitful. You are already clean because of the word I have spoken to you."

Jesus was giving us a living parable. The Father is always at work in our lives. He loves us perfectly, and too perfectly to leave us so imperfect. We are predestined to be conformed to the likeness of Jesus, and he will see that this happens. For those Followers who have drifted, or have become lukewarm, or find themselves covered with lazy dust, he will lift them up, and dust them off, so the Son can shine on and through them – producing fruit again.

For those Followers who are already actively bearing fruit through their reliance on the Holy Spirit's power, he prunes off the unnecessary leaves so they may thrive and flourish, bearing even more fruit. It is a constant process. One for which I am so grateful. In so many of my prayers I ask the Father, "Please, do not ever let up on me. Prune me whenever I need pruning. Sift me whenever I need sifting. I want everything you want for me. I do not want to miss a thing!"

The Holy Spirit prompted the writer of Hebrews to write it his way:

> "My son, do not make light of the Lord's discipline,
> and do not lose heart when he rebukes you,
> because the Lord disciplines the one he loves,
> and he chastens everyone he accepts as his son."
> (From Proverbs)

> Endure hardship as discipline; God is treating you as his children. For what children are not disciplined by their father? If you are not disciplined—and everyone undergoes discipline—then you are not legitimate, not true sons and daughters at all. Moreover, we have all had human fathers who disciplined us

> and we respected them for it. How much more should we submit to the Father of spirits and live!
>
> They disciplined us for a little while as they thought best; but God disciplines us for our good, in order that we may share in his holiness. No discipline seems pleasant at the time, but painful. Later on, however, it produces a harvest of righteousness and peace for those who have been trained by it.

"A harvest of righteousness and peace for those who have been trained for it" ... by lifting up, pruning and sifting.

Jesus paused for a moment, looking at the vine intently, then continued,

> "Remain in me, as I also remain in you. No branch can bear fruit by itself; it must remain in the vine. Neither can you bear fruit unless you remain in me. I am the vine; you are the branches. If you remain in me and I in you, you will bear much fruit; apart from me you can do nothing."
>
> "My command is this: Love each other as I have loved you. Greater love has no one than this: to lay down one's life for one's friends. You are my friends if you do what I command. I no longer call you servants, because a servant does not know his master's business. Instead, I have called you friends, for everything that I learned from my Father I have made known to you.
>
> "When the Advocate comes, whom I will send to you from the Father—the Spirit of truth who goes out from the Father—he will testify about me. And you also must testify, for you have been with me from the beginning.
>
> "I have much more to say to you, more than you can now bear. But when he, the Spirit of truth,

> comes, he will guide you into all the truth. He will not speak on his own; he will speak only what he hears, and he will tell you what is yet to come. He will glorify me because it is from me that he will receive what he will make known to you. All that belongs to the Father is mine. That is why I said the Spirit will receive from me what he will make known to you."

As we passed through the vineyard Jesus stopped. He raised his arms and lifted his face towards the sky, and suddenly began to pray. He prayed to his Father, for himself, for us, and for you, the future Family of Followers. It is a beautiful, majestic prayer, and I have recorded it in my gospel. He captured my heart at the beginning of his prayer when he said,

> "Father, the hour has come. Glorify your Son, that your Son may glorify you. For you granted him authority over all people that he might give eternal life to all those you have given him. Now this is eternal life: that they know you, the only true God, and Jesus Christ, whom you have sent."

Eternal life – now – beginning right this minute, as you read these words. And it is all about knowing God Almighty, El Shaddai, as your loving Heavenly Father, and Jesus as your Lord, your Savior, and your best friend. To know the Father as Abba; to experience him in the day-to-day details and circumstances and relationships of your life, is to be living 'Heaven on earth' now.

Please do not miss that 'best friend' part, too. Jesus told us that night we were no longer just disciples, who followed him around, we were now *friends*. It dug deep into my soul that night and sustained me for the days and years to come. My best friend.

And that is what Jesus is. His love is perfect, penetrating, and powerful. There is simply nothing like it.

And yet his friendship takes the relationship to another level. I can turn to him. I can talk to him – as a friend. I know he hears me – as a friend. I know he understands me – as a friend. I know he loves me. And please do not miss this: I know he likes me. Yes, me, with all my flaws.

Perhaps this is why I call myself, "The disciple whom Jesus loved." As I said much earlier, I do not think Jesus loved me more than the other disciples. For that matter, I do not think he loves me more than he loves you. No, it is not about the quantity of his love; it is about the quality.

As we go deeper in our friendship with him, we come to know the Father, and eternal life is then in full swing. Here. Now. Life in the flow of the Kingdom among us. Is there anything holding you back from this?

If there is, I can tell you who it is: you. Satan cannot hold you back. The culture or the world around you cannot. Even sin cannot. Only you, my friend. So start right now dying to that sorry old Self, and surrendering to the new eternal life, life to the full.

35

"IT IS FINISHED!"

John 19

We crossed the Kidron Valley and arrived at one of Jesus' favorite places: an olive grove called Gethsemane, on the side of the Mount of Olives, looking back to Jerusalem. While we were, there he motioned for Simon, my brother, James, and me to follow him as he slipped away from the others. They had all fallen asleep at this point.

But please go easy on them, and us, for falling asleep. We had been at the Seder meal for four hours and had drunk four cups of wine. It was late, and we were all exhausted.

The three of us followed him for a short distance into the olive trees. After a moment Jesus stopped, looked around, and then told us to sit down and wait on him, because he wanted to pray. He walked a few paces more, then suddenly collapsed onto his knees with his face to the ground, and began to pray. He was clearly conflicted - anguished, actually. I could barely hear what he was saying. He prayed three different times:

> "My Father, if it is possible, may this cup be taken from me. Yet not as I will, but as you will."

Jesus returned to us and found us sleeping. "Couldn't you men keep watch with me for one hour?" he asked Simon Peter. Then he said to us, "My soul is overwhelmed with sorrow to the point of death. Watch and pray so that you will not fall into temptation. The spirit is willing, but the flesh is weak."

We were so tired and confused. That night is still somewhat of a blur to me, but I believe Jesus was saying to us, "My Spirit is willing, I will do whatever the Father asks of me, even unto death. But my humanity is weakened right now, and I want your support and companionship. Stay up with me and join me in my time of prayer, please."

The third time he returned to us his mood had shifted. Gone was the trepidation; he was purposeful and undaunted. He looked into the darkness and said to us, "Are you still sleeping? Look, the hour has come, and the Son of Man is delivered into the hands of sinners. Rise! Let us go! Here comes my betrayer!

PILATE'S POWER?

Matthew, Mark, and Dr. Luke give very detailed accounts of Jesus' arrest, and the following trial and crucifixion. Please read their accounts, as I do not care to relive that horrible experience with you. I will only include one exchange between Pilate and Jesus.

Jesus had already been flogged. He was a bloody mess. Most of the life had been beaten out of him. Or so they thought. Yet even then, he stood straight and looked Pilate in the eye as Pilate continued to question him. This truly unnerved Pilate. He was a hard and ruthless man, but this Jesus, this bloodied man, whom he knew was innocent, was acting as if he was in control – as if he owned the place. Here is the exchange:

> The Jewish leaders insisted, "We have a law, and according to that law he must die, because he claimed to be the Son of God."

> When Pilate heard this, he was even more afraid, and he went back inside the palace. "Where do you come from?" he asked Jesus, but Jesus gave him no answer. "Do you refuse to speak to me?" Pilate said. "Don't you realize I have power either to free you or to crucify you?"

Jesus looked Pilate directly in the eye and simply stated,

> "You would have no power over me if it were not given to you from above."

This truth governed Jesus' life. I encourage you to let this same truth, the Father's total control, govern yours. Nothing happens to you that your Heavenly Father – who loves you perfectly – has not allowed. Once, during a particularly trying time, I asked Saul, Simon and Jesus' brother James, if they thought the current trial was from God or from Satan. The three men pondered my question for a moment, then James looked up and smiled and said, "Yes!"

His message was clear. What does it matter? My Heavenly Father allowed it, at the very least, and he may have even caused it. Or as so often happens, allowed me to cause it. Either way, "You would have no power over me if it were not given from above." Jesus' own words in Matthew's account give us instant clarity on this:

> "Do not be afraid of those who kill the body but cannot kill the soul. Rather, be afraid of the One who can destroy both soul and body in hell. Are not two sparrows sold for a penny? Yet not one of them will fall to the ground outside your Father's care. And even the very hairs of your head are all numbered. So don't be afraid; you are worth more than many sparrows."

Jesus' matter-of-fact response to Pilate – "You would have no power over me …" - rattled him. I have seen the Master's expressions as he interacted with people, and I can picture his expression when he said this to Pilate. He would not have smirked or condescended, but Pilate would have known he was out of his league, and that he was in the presence of true greatness. He would have felt exposed.

Remember, once again, the cross did not happen to Jesus; Jesus happened to the cross. He was not a victim; he was the Victor.

And Pilate knew it.

Pilate and the Jewish authorities were the actual victims. Victims of their own Self-interests, and victims of Jesus' refusal to back down to them.

After Jesus' death on the cross, Joseph of Arimathea and Nicodemus took Jesus' body down off the cross and prepared it for burial. It was a touching show of affection, and a dangerous one. These two men of the Sanhedrin were risking their reputations, their standing with the other Jewish authorities, and possibly even their lives. But Jesus had touched something inside each of them, something akin to deep calling unto deep.

HE IS ALIVE!

A few months after the whole Passover crucifixion happened, Nicodemus sought me out and asked me to give him a full account of Jesus' appearances after his resurrection. He recognized our eyewitness testimony was compelling, but he had also heard what appeared to be conflicting reports about Jesus' resurrection appearances that first day. Some of the Apostles talked about there being one angel, and others two angels at the grave. (There were two, but only one spoke.) Others have mentioned different women who went to the tomb early that morning.

These and any other apparent contradictions can easily be explained. I use the word 'apparent,' because that is what they are. I have observed over the years that when different people talk about the same event, they tend to emphasize different details. The central story is the same, but they tend to mention the particular details that made an impression on them and leave out others.

To me, these differences make our story more valid, not less. These small differences in detail prove we did not get together to make up our story. If we had, we would have been sure to be more consistent. (And perhaps we would have left out the many parts that made us look stupid and cowardly.)

But we never did anything of the kind. These differences are simply a matter of perspective. Different perspectives emphasize different details. But when the essence of the story is the same, and the overall storyline is consistent, any differences confirm the validity of the story.

Rest assured, we did not follow cleverly devised stories when we told you about the coming of our Lord Jesus Christ in power, but we were eyewitnesses of his majesty. He received honor and glory from God the Father when the voice came to him from the Majestic Glory, saying, "This is my Son, whom I love; with him I am well pleased." We ourselves heard this voice that came from heaven when we were with him on the sacred mountain.

We also have the prophetic message as something completely reliable, and you will do well to pay attention to it. Above all, you must understand that no prophecy of Scripture came about by the prophet's own interpretation of things. For prophecy never had its origin in the human will, but prophets, though human, spoke from God as they were carried along by the Holy Spirit.

So I shared with Nicodemus exactly how it happened that fateful morning, when everything changed in our lives - forever. I gave him a much more detailed account, but since I am sure by now you have heard much about this, I will just give you the bare facts.

Mary Magdalene and the other women went to the tomb early that morning hoping to anoint Jesus' body. When they arrived, they saw the tomb was open and empty. Mary Magdalene left immediately to find me, while the other women remained, somewhat dumbfounded.

Simon Peter was with me at the time, although Mary did not know this. I had found my dear friend curled up in an alley, drowning in tears of the agony of his betrayal. I had gone looking for him to comfort him. I knew he was devastated and ashamed.

Mary found us and in between her gasping breaths she exclaimed, "Come see, the tomb is empty!" Simon looked at me bewildered, but soon a smile crept across his face. He knew what this meant. So did I. But could it be? Could this really mean Jesus was alive?

Without saying another word, we took off running. Mary followed us, but she could not possibly keep up with us. As soon as we arrived, we both stepped into the tomb to verify it was empty. Confused, but excited, we left to go tell the other brothers what had happened. To say our hearts were racing would be an understatement.

Can you only imagine?

HE CALLED ME BY NAME

Mary arrived at the tomb just as we were leaving, and she stayed behind. When we saw her again she told us what happened next. She said she saw two angels, one of whom spoke to her. Then, as she turned to leave, she saw Jesus. She did not recognize him until he called her by name, "Mary."

She said the instant she heard her name she recognized his voice. How many times have I seen this play out with so many different people? When Jesus calls your name, you know it. There can be no mistaking it. And even now, when I hear his voice calling my name, my heart, just as Mary's heart, lights up with joy.

After Jesus spoke to Mary, she left to tell the disciples. About that same time, Simon and I were walking back into the city. Simon Peter told me he needed a few minutes alone, to gather himself before seeing the other disciples. That is when Jesus appeared to him.

Peter told me later that Jesus didn't say much. He just smiled and said he loved him, and that things were happening just as he had told us, and just as the Father had planned. He also smiled and said, "And Peter, my little rock, all is well with us. You are still my beloved friend. And I still have a plan for you." With that he motioned for Simon to go and join the other disciples, and he disappeared.

Meanwhile, the other women then encountered two angels on their way to see us. One of the angels told them, "He is not here; he has risen … Go quickly and tell his disciples: 'He has risen from the dead and is going ahead of you into Galilee.'" They started on their way back into the city, and along the way Jesus appeared to them, too. He told them the same thing the angel had. When they arrived, they told the disciples what they had seen. You can imagine the men were very confused.

Jesus appeared to two other disciples that same afternoon. Cleopas and Thaddeus left Jerusalem and the other disciples earlier that day for their home in Emmaus. You can read about their encounter with Jesus in Dr. Luke's account. Afterward, they hurried back to tell us they had seen the risen Lord. Simon and I had rejoined the other disciples at this point. Later that day Jesus appeared to all of us, but Thomas was not there.

A week later Jesus appeared to us again, and this time with Thomas present.

After this we all returned to Galilee, just as Jesus had told us to do. While we were in Galilee, Jesus appeared to us several times, teaching and talking about the Kingdom of God. Once, when we were headed to the mountain to pray and seek Jesus, as he had instructed us to do, a crowd began to follow us. With the word spreading that we were expecting to see Jesus again, the crowd swelled to at least five hundred. They all wanted to see this risen Messiah, who had lived and taught in their towns and villages.

That day he gave us his great commission, to go and make disciples throughout the world:

> "All authority in heaven and on earth has been given to me. Therefore go and make disciples of all nations, baptizing them in the name of the Father and of the Son and of the Holy Spirit, and teaching them to obey everything I have commanded you. And surely I am with you always, to the very end of the age."

During this Galilean time, Jesus appeared to James privately, restoring him as well, and making clear his role in the future Jerusalem Family of Followers. Later we all went back to Jerusalem, Jesus' family included, for the Feast of Pentecost. During this time we met Jesus on the Mount of Olives for his final ascension.

Saul sums this up nicely in his first letter to the Followers in Corinth:

> For what I received I passed on to you as of first importance: that Christ died for our sins according to the Scriptures, that he was buried, that he was raised on the third day according to the Scriptures, and that he appeared to Cephas, and then to the Twelve. After that, he appeared to more than five hundred of the brothers and sisters at the same time, most of whom are still living, though some have fallen asleep. Then he appeared to James, then to all the apostles, and last of all he appeared to me also, as to one abnormally born.

Many of those five hundred have now passed on by this time of my writing, but some are still around. Go ask them. They witnessed it, too!

36

BREAKFAST ON THE BEACH

John 21

As I said, I will not describe the events of Jesus' last week in Jerusalem, or his gruesome crucifixion. You can read about those in the other Gospel accounts. I simply do not have the stomach to describe it all. I do not wish to relive that time. It is simply too painful. Even with Jesus' triumphal resurrection, watching my dear friend suffer so is just too much for me to revisit.

But before I finish, I want to tell you about one last encounter – the time I mentioned at the outset of this story, when Jesus appeared to us after a night of fishing. I believe it is a fitting conclusion to my … to our … to his … story.

This happened during the forty days during which Jesus made several appearances to us. It happened this way: Simon Peter, Thomas (also known as Didymus), Nathanael, brother James and I, and two other disciples were together. "I'm going out to fish," Simon told us. Simon could not sit still any longer. He was a can-do kind of man, therefore activity, any activity, was better than sitting around and waiting.

But we were ready for a change, too, so we eagerly agreed. We prepared our nets and got into our boat, but that night we caught nothing. During our fruitless night of fishing I began to wonder if we were doing the right thing. Fishing is innocent enough, but were we edging closer to returning to our old way of life – leaning on our own provision?

Perhaps our utter failure that night was the Master's way of showing us we would never be fishers of fish again. Early in the morning, as we were making our way back to shore, there was a man on the shore with a fire going. The smell of fresh fish cooking wafted across the water, causing my stomach to lurch, reminding me how hungry I was.

He called out to us, "Friends, haven't you any fish?" "No," we answered. I thought it was a strange question. He already had fish on his fire. Was he wanting to buy more fish? Or just being friendly?

He then pointed to the right side of our boat and shouted, "Throw your net on the right side of the boat and you will find some." Simon looked at the rest of us with a quizzical look, shrugged his shoulders and said, "Why not?" For whatever reason we did not even discuss it, we just cast the nets out, once again.

When we did, we were unable to haul the net in because of the large number of fish. It was as if the fish were on a mission to jump into our nets. In all my days of fishing I had never seen anything like this. And there was nothing but large fish. No small throw-back fish, as would be normal.

We were working so hard, yet the fish seemed to be helping us. They were popping up out of the water as if they wanted to be a part of this miracle. James was shouting for us to work together, and to be sure not to break the nets. Nathanael and Thomas were scurrying around the boat. It was a frantic moment. In the midst of the chaos, I stood up and again looked to the shore.

Then my stomach lurched again. I was immediately transported back in time to that early encounter on the beach, all that time ago, when Jesus told Simon to push his boat out a little deeper. Again, after a fruitless night of fishing:

Jesus had been preaching from Simon's boat, and the resulting catch was so huge that Simon fell to his knees and cried out, "Go away from me, Lord; I am a sinful man!"

I grabbed Simon and cried out, "It is the Lord!" As soon as Simon Peter heard me say it, almost before I finished, he wrapped his outer garment around him (for he had taken it off) and jumped into the water. He is impetuous! As he swam to shore we followed in the boat, towing the net full of fish, for we were not far from shore, only about a hundred yards.

If I could have carried that boat on my shoulders, I would have. If I could have walked on water, I would have. I could not get there fast enough. Suddenly joy flooded my heart as I realized just how much I had missed him. When we landed, we saw the fire of burning coals with the fish grilling.

Jesus hugged each of us, and then laughed and said, "Bring some of the fish you have just caught." So Simon Peter climbed back into the boat and helped us drag the net ashore. We needed all the help we could get because it was full of large fish, 153, to be exact. But even with so many, the net was not torn. Jesus sat down next to the fire, opened his arms and said, "Come and have breakfast."

He was as natural as if this was just another normal day in our three-year journey with him. None of the disciples dared ask him, "Who are you?" We knew it was the Lord. But it was not just the Lord. It was the resurrected Lord. Jesus then took the bread and passed it around, and he did the same with the fish. This was now the third time Jesus appeared to us personally, just us, after he was raised from the dead.

As we ate, we talked about our fishing expedition. We all made a point to single out just whose idea it was. Simon tried to deflect, but we were having such a good time it did not really matter. The morning sun was bright, but soft and warming. Especially after having been on the water all night. The smell of the fish and the fire relaxed every bone in my body. A warm breeze floated across us. Maybe it was the Holy Spirit?

It was nice just to be with Jesus. This was a memory I would cherish all the days of my life. Just us. Together, once again, laughing, relaxing, chatting and having fun. If I could have frozen time for all eternity I would have. This had to be a foretaste of Heaven. We knew things would never be the same. Jesus was with us as before, yes, yet we knew his resurrection had changed everything. But for this morning, sitting on the beach with the warm sun on our faces and the sound of the sizzling fish cooking over the fire, none of that mattered.

My lasting memory of these times with the Master was just how much he enjoyed being with us. He was as relaxed as I had ever seen him. But I want you to know I have continued to live with this same relationship all these years. Of course, my interaction with my best friend and Lord is different, now that he is not with me physically, but, and you may not believe this, now it is even better.

PULL UP A CHAIR

He told us it would be better. On his last night with us he told us the Holy Spirit would come, and the Holy Spirit would in fact make it better. And he was right. Now, whenever I feel any sense of loneliness or despair, or worry or fear, I pull a chair up beside me and I talk with Jesus, as if he is sitting in the chair right next to me. Because he is.

I am rarely lonely, and I have learned to be content in any and every circumstance. But on those occasions when my feelings try to take over, I just start talking with Jesus. You can do this too, my friend. This is not just for apostles, or super-Christians. It is for you. It is for everyone who has surrendered to the Master, been born again and set free.

Just pull up a chair and talk with your best friend.

I recall when Jesus' mother, Mary, died. I felt so lonely. I had been caring for her since the cross, and she had become like a mother to me. Her loss took me back to losing Jesus, and I could not shake this overwhelming sense of despair. I had this huge hole inside. It was awful.

So in that moment, instead of seeking someone to comfort me, I sat down on the floor, and said, "Jesus, I need you right now. The hole inside me is about to undo me. I am aching with pain, and I need you to fill me, right now, with your presence, and your perfect love. And I am not getting off this floor until you do."

And he did. Of course he did. That is what he said he would do, and who he said he is: a compassionate and loving friend. And he has done it many other times. He will do this for you, too. He is always with you. He understands every emotion you are experiencing. His compassion for you, his love for you, and his devotion to you will never waver.

I love the way the writer of Hebrews put it,

> Therefore, since we have a great high priest who has ascended into heaven, Jesus the Son of God, let us hold firmly to the faith we profess. For we do not have a high priest who is unable to empathize with our weaknesses, but we have one who has been tempted in every way, just as we are—yet he did not sin. Let us then approach God's throne of grace with confidence, so that we may receive mercy and find grace to help us in our time of need.

Do you see that in all Jesus' post-resurrection appearances, Jesus was seeking us out? He was not waiting for us to come around, to come to our senses. He did not wait for us to repent of our abandoning him. He did not wait for us to come groveling back to him. He did exactly what the father did with his wayward son in Jesus' parable in Luke's gospel: He jumped off that porch and he met us where we were: broken, dispirited, sad and discouraged.

He sought us out; he found us; he redeemed us.

And Jesus will do this with you as well. He initiates all. He calls us by name. Just as the Father is described in Chronicles:

> For the eyes of the LORD range throughout the earth to strengthen those whose hearts are fully committed to him.

Remember,
God loves you.
He's on your side.
He's coming after you.
He is relentless.

37

A FINAL WALK TOGETHER

When we had finished eating, Jesus pulled Simon Peter aside and motioned for him to walk with him. They both stood up and started down the beach. The rest of us could see Jesus wanted some time alone with Simon, so we just sat back, enjoying the warmth of the sun on our faces. Simon later described to me what happened next.

They walked a few paces, then Jesus stopped, looked back at the fishing gear, the nets still bursting with fish, and said, "Simon son of John, do you love me, deeply and unconditionally, more than these?" He was pointing toward the fishing gear. The point of the question was crystal clear: Is it going to be me you follow from now on, or your old, familiar way of life?

Remember, the Master never asked a question looking for information. He wanted Simon to think deeply about what he wanted in life from this point forward. He told us we could not serve two masters, and he wanted Simon to fully face this truth. Would Jesus, with all the coming uncertainty and danger involved, be his Master, or would the comfort and safety of his old life of fishing prevail?

And notice he called him Simon, not Peter. Do not miss that. He was taking Simon back to the very beginning. After his spectacular denial of Jesus, it was time to start over. To be stripped down and reclothed.

"Yes, Lord," Simon replied, "you know that you are like a brother to me."

Jesus had asked Simon if he loved him, fully and unconditionally – *agapeo* in the Greek – but Simon had answered with 'phileo,' brotherly love. Of course, as two Jewish men they were speaking Aramaic to each other, but I have chosen these Greek words to best represent their meaning.

Jesus ignored this sidestep by Simon, this deflection, and said, "Feed my lambs."

They walked a little further and again Jesus said, "Simon son of John, do you love me?" Jesus hesitated and then continued, "fully and unconditionally?"

Simon shifted a little, looked down at the sand, and answered, "Yes, Lord, you know that I love you like a dear brother."

Jesus was undaunted by Simon's second deflection. He was going to dig down to the foundation with Simon until he broke through. He said, "Take care of my sheep." They started to walk again, but Jesus stooped down and picked up a shell and tossed it into the water. The shell skipped and disturbed a bird floating on the surface. He looked at the sky as a flock of birds flew by, and then slowly turned to Simon.

The third time he said to him, "Simon, son of John, do you even love me like a brother?"

Peter was hurt because Jesus asked him the third time, "Do you love me?" But this time the Master lowered the bar down to Simon's previous lukewarm responses. It is as if Jesus was saying, "Okay Simon, if you cannot bring yourself to state unequivocally, 'I love you unconditionally,' are you so sure you can even say you like me, as a brother?"

To be fair to Simon, he was in a tenuous situation. Or at least he thought he was. Aside from Jesus' brief appearance after we discovered the empty tomb, this was his first one-on-one encounter with Jesus since he had so vehemently and blatantly denied him – with swearing oaths, mind you. Peter later confided in me that he just could not bring himself to state anything emphatically with any confidence. He was on unsteady ground, and so he was guarded with his responses. (Something we never need to be with Jesus)

Remember, he knows all about you. Your frailties, your fragility, your humanness. And he still loves you. This was his purpose with Simon that day. To bring him face to face with his failure, and to then assure him it was all right between them. To assure this defeated and devastated man that he was still loved perfectly, and that he was forgiven, completely.

After Jesus' third question, Simon stopped and slowly looked up into Jesus' eyes. A silence fell between them. Eternity may have passed between them in that moment - it was deep calling unto deep. Finally, Simon slowly said, "Lord, you know all things; you know that I am doing my best to love you fully and unconditionally. But I cannot even do that without you helping me."

And with that Jesus had accomplished what he set out to do. He had stripped Simon of his silly pride and was now ready to build him back up. But not to the previous, Self-made man. No, he was building him into a new Holy Spirit-made man. With a mission to feed his sheep, to take care of his flock, and to lead. But now he would lead as a servant leader.

Jesus knew Simon Peter would be the leader of The Twelve moving forward. But the old Simon knew only one way to lead, or for that matter one way to accomplish anything: Power up. Certainly not to power down - ever. His Self could only lead by force – often the sheer force of his size and his mouth and his bombastic personality. For Simon, it was, "If I don't, it won't. If it's to be, it's up to me!"

This would never work moving forward, advancing the Kingdom into the world. Simon had to be sifted, just as Jesus had said during our last supper together. He had to have the props knocked out from under him. All those things that propped up his ego and his sense of Self.

It was not pretty, and it was not painless. But it was absolutely necessary. I pray the Father never lets up on me, either. Even to this day I need to be sifted. And so do you.

"WHAT IS THAT TO YOU? YOU FOLLOW ME."

Jesus then said, "Feed my sheep." He looked out over the water, raising his hands and saying, "Very truly I tell you, when you were younger you dressed yourself and went where you wanted; but when you are old you will stretch out your hands, and someone else will dress you and lead you where you do not want to go."

Jesus said this to indicate the kind of death by which Peter would glorify God. Then he said to him, "Follow me!"

By this time, for some reason I cannot explain, I began to follow them down the beach. Simon turned and saw me following them. He turned to Jesus and asked, "Lord, what about him?"

Jesus answered, "If I want him to remain alive until I return, what is that to you? You must follow me." Now because of this, the rumor spread among the believers that I would not die. I have, in fact, outlived all my fellow apostles. But Jesus did not say that I would not die; he only said, "If I want him to remain alive until I return, what is that to you?"

"What is that to you? You follow me." These final words of Jesus to Simon perfectly capture the path for all of us.

Amidst all the chaos that can and will surround us, the message to each of us from Jesus is, "What is that to you? You follow me." Lately, I find myself becoming distracted by questions such as, "How can emperors such as Nero and Domitian, as evil as they are, be in charge of the world?" Or, "What is going to become of our new Way?"

But Jesus offers a simple answer: "John, my son, you follow me."

He offers this simple answer to you as well.

Jesus, the master communicator, is bringing our focus back from the swirling world around us, to ourselves – to me, and to you. Not others, not the events taking place around you – you. Because you, and your inward workings with Jesus, are all that is eternal in this world.

In this, his final walk-and-talk with Simon on the beach, Jesus was driving home to Simon that his mission, for the rest of his life, would be to take care of Jesus' followers. Jesus told him this three times so there could be no confusion in Simon's mind, and certainly no distractions from his central mission.

It is as if Jesus is saying, "Simon, I know you bounce around a lot and are easily distracted, so I want to be absolutely clear: Your mission in life, above all else, is to take care of my growing Family of Followers. Is that clear, Simon? Three times clear?"

One would assume Jesus had Simon's rapt attention. But … Simon is aware that I am following them, so he becomes distracted. I could see the incredulous look on Jesus' face when he said, "What is that to you? You must follow me."

Could Simon not keep his focus for one minute? He is walking one-on-one with the Savior of the world. He is walking with his dear friend whom he has seen dead and now alive, and yet he cannot help but ask questions about someone else. But he is not that different from you and me. We are so easily distracted. We so easily lose focus on what really matters, and get sidetracked over other people, other events, and other issues.

I am sure for some of you there is real chaos in your personal lives. I know it is very real and very scary for you. I also know Jesus cares, deeply and intimately, and he will listen to all your concerns and worries as long as you want to share them with him. He will do so with sincerity and compassion. And yet, with all appropriate sensitivity, I think he would eventually smile lovingly and still say,

"What is that to you? You follow me."

Not: Follow doctrine. Not: Follow the rabbis. Not: Follow the Apostles. And certainly not: Follow the culture.

Jesus is saying to me and to you:

"You do not need to worry about all this chaos – Keep your focus on me."

"When your faith wobbles because your feelings are taking over, just remember, keep your eyes on me. For I am the way, the truth and the life. *You* ... follow me.'"

NO LOOKING BACK AT SINS OR WINS

Recall how Jesus so masterfully restored the Samaritan woman at the well, and the young woman caught in adultery. For the Followers of Jesus, there is no looking back at our failures and defeats. Because in the Kingdom they are not failures, and they are not defeats. They are mere setbacks along the way, opportunities for repentance and adjustments. Do not ever forget that there is now no condemnation for those who have surrendered their lives to the King.

Saul said it this way in his letter to the Followers in Philippi:

> Not that I have already obtained all this, or have already arrived at my goal, but I press on to take hold of that for which Christ Jesus took hold of me. Brothers and sisters, I do not consider myself yet to have taken hold of it.
>
> But one thing I do: Forgetting what is behind and straining toward what is ahead, I press on toward the goal to win the prize for which God has called me heavenward in Christ Jesus.

For the follower of Jesus, there is no point in looking back at our sins or our wins. One beats us down, the other pumps us up. We press on toward his goal for us, because we are God's workmanship, created in Christ Jesus to do good works, which God has prepared in advance for us to do. Whatever sins you have in your past, my friend, after you are born again, God has removed them as far as the east is from the west, and you are now holy and blameless in his sight, without blemish, and free from accusation.

The only person who will turn you backward is the accuser, Satan. Do not let him. Resist him and he will flee from you. Jesus is calling you forward to a bright and joyful future with him!

UNTIL WE MEET AGAIN

From my first encounter with the Master by the Jordan River, with John the Baptizer, to that first day on the beach, when we dropped our nets to follow him, my life has changed in so many ways. My brother James was beheaded. Stephen was stoned. Peter was crucified upside down by Nero, and Saul was beheaded by that same mad tyrant. I have lost so many so dear to me. Their loss is bittersweet. Yet I have gained so many Brothers and Sisters in our Family of Followers, and that joy has been overwhelmingly, wonderfully, sweet.

But one thing remained the same through the years, consistent and steady as the sun and the moon, even to this day: His love for me. Through thin and flush, sadness and joy – mostly flush and mostly joy – he has been my constant companion. I know I will see him soon. My days in this body are numbered. But when I see my Lord, it will not be a reunion, for he has never left me. We will simply continue whatever conversation we are having as I pass from this world to his world. As a matter of fact, I may not realize I am dead for a few days!

For ours is a conversational walk through life, talking with one another about what we are doing together. I will soon see his warm and encouraging smile. I will soon feel his hand on my back, again. James, along with Father and Mother, will greet me. Simon Peter will grab me and lift me up. Saul will want to discuss the finer points of theology. Mary will smile her shy smile and say, "Welcome home, my adopted son."

Nicodemus will laugh with me about his first, awkward, but life-changing encounter with Jesus. The Samaritan woman at the well will throw her arms open and hug me, and hand me a jar of living water. The royal official will greet me with a wink, and say, "You remember, I took him at his word."

The lame man will jump up and down and dance a jig with me. The man born blind will open his eyes wide in mock surprise and laugh with me. Lazarus, Mary, and Martha will be planning a dinner in honor of my arrival. Perhaps they will pick fruit and vegetables from the Tree of Life. Oh, how I look forward to those feasts in heaven.

But when I see Jesus, my best friend, my Master, my Savior, my joy will be complete. One joyous Family, now all together, for eternity. I hope you will join us. In our Family there are no good-byes, only "God be with you," until I see you again. So my dear friend, until we meet again,

The LORD bless you
  and keep you;
the LORD make his face shine on you
  and be gracious to you;
the LORD turn his face toward you
  and give you peace.

CITATIONS AND CREDITS

Chapter	Quotation	By
1 / 18	A conversational walk through life …	Dallas Willard
4	Jewish Education System	Brad Gray
9	Water to wine	Doug Greenwold
	Tuesday wedding day	TPT Notes
10	Who God is – How He does things- What He cares about	Doug Greenwold
	Calm Relaxed Pace	Oswald Chambers
14	John 10:21	MSG
16 / 36	God loves you – He is on your side	Eugene Peterson Funeral: Son's Eulogy
	Three-Fold sin management system	Doug Greenwold
17	"Jesus pointed down onto the well …"	TPT
	"All you thirsty ones …"	TPT
20	Evangelism is as Simple as 1-2-3	Search Ministries
22	You may believe in Jesus, but do you believe what Jesus believed	John Ortberg
	"If you have a purpose of your own …"	Oswald Chambers

23	The Rabbi and the Roman Guard	Brad Gray
27	I Want to See scripture	MSG
	If all you see is what you see then you are …	Tony Evans
30	Lord, Liar, Lunatic forms the basis for my discussion	C.S. Lewis
	"The value of our public service flows from …"	Oswald Chambers
31	Four Day Faith	Doug Greenwold
	To glorify means to accurately reveal	Doug Greenwold
	Satan's 3 D's	Search Ministries
32	John bar Barr ending to chapter	John Barr *Waylaid by the Light*
33	Triclinium Table	Brad Gray
34	"I will not leave you orphaned …"	MSG
37	"I may not realize I am dead for a few days "	Dallas Willard

Made in the USA
Middletown, DE
03 July 2023

34358474R00184